Seven Letters
That Will Bring You Closer to Your College Student

Seven Letters
That Will Bring You Closer to Your College Student

Steven M Harris
Roy A. Bean

Provo, Utah

Printed by Y Mountain Press

Contents

Dear Parents,

As I am about to send my son Sam off to college, I am struck by how fast time goes in a parent-child relationship and by how much that relationship changes from birth through the teen years. I'd like to think that I have said and done all the right things with him during his child-hood, but I am pretty sure that is not possible. Still, I look forward to developing a new relationship with Sam as he starts college and grows into a young adult.

Going to college was a big decision for my son, as it is for so many young people. And they all need our support. Sometimes that can come in the form of some kind and reassuring words. Sometimes it comes as a simple pat on the back and a gentle nudge forward – encouraging them to expand their freedom to choose their own path, make their own choices, and have their own successes and failures.

In the College of Education and Human Development, we pride ourselves in supporting each other and encouraging exploration and discovery throughout our community. We know that a student's time in college provides an incredible opportunity for growth and maturity. I encourage you to consider following the advice of this book, which offers you a process for communicating and supporting your children during their college years. It's an example of the kind of human development research and community building activity that happens throughout our college and the University of Minnesota.

We look forward to assisting your students on their college journey, and we want to keep the lines of communication open with them and with you throughout.

Best wishes,

Jean K. Quam, Ph.D., Dean
College of Education and Human Development
University of Minnesota

Introduction

Have you been to a bookstore lately to find books on getting your son or daughter ready for college? There are many books that are informative and helpful. You can find information on choosing a school, selecting a major, improving your child's standardized test scores, finding financial aid, and the list goes on. However, the bottom line is that most books focus only on preparing your child for the college experience, and do little to help you with the transition.

You've had 18 years or more to be a direct and dramatic influence in the life of your child. So, now that your child is moving away, you just have to give that up? Obviously not (especially for those of you who are still writing the checks). When your son or daughter goes to college—whether he or she attends a school across the country or takes courses at a local campus while living at home—you are beginning a new chapter in your relationship. You don't stop being a parent when your kid moves away or attends school. However, the available college preparation books don't say anything about how you can maintain or, better yet, strengthen · your relationship with your child during this phase of life.

There is very little in these books that address parents' deep desire to stay close to their children. Through the college experience, you will get to know your child in a whole new way that acknowledges your child's growth and maturity and redefines what it means to be connected as parent and child. As a parent, you want to stay close to your child because your family bonds are strong, even if your relationships aren't perfect. We believe that this is a worthy goal – one deserving of support and assistance. In fact, we have written this book to provide you with specific tools and concrete suggestions on how to strengthen the parent-child relationship while your child is in college.

The absence of literature on this topic indicates that

this has been a neglected area of social research. There are volumes upon volumes of information dedicated to helping parents toilet train their children or deal with tantrums, for example, but relatively little guidance for negotiating that awkward (but sometimes magical) time when your child is no longer a child but is not quite ready to be fully considered an adult.

Navigating this developmental stage can be difficult for parents. At one end of the spectrum, some parents relinquish most of their parental responsibility, providing money, as they are capable, but forgetting that they can still play a meaningful role in the guidance of their children. At the opposite end of the spectrum, other parents seem to think of their kids as they appeared in their baby pictures: dependent and helpless. These are the "helicopter parents" that give college administrators fits. More importantly, when parents treat their children this way they do little to foster meaningful adult-to-adult relationships.

Children need to see their parents as human beings, not as demons or angels.

Successfully negotiating this developmental transition hinges on both parties changing their perspectives. Children need to begin to see their parents as human beings, not as demons or angels. They need to get to a point where they can go to their parents for advice or guidance—not because they have to, but because they know that their parents will always have their best inter-

Your letters will invite conversation, enhance understanding, and foster deeper emotional connection.

ests at heart. They need to see the value of their parents' perspective. Parents also need to see their children in a different way. Children can no longer be viewed as helpless or in need of constant guidance; rather, parents need to see them as adults, capable of making wise choices that may not always reflect what the parent would have them do. If neither children nor parents can learn this new way of seeing each other, it is harder for a secure long-term relationship to develop between adult children and their parents.

It is our hope that this book will help you strengthen the relationship you have with your college student. While some of you may be thinking that you are already pretty close to your college student—you talk with each other every day, and you know his or her class schedule, roommates, and cafeteria menu—we are talking about creating an even more meaningful and important relationship. Others reading this might think that they are not very close to their college student and that they've tried to have meaningful conversations, but they always end up in an argument. If done correctly, the method we propose in this book avoids contention and focuses attention on the relationship without distractions. Our method invites further conversations, enhances understanding, and fosters deeper emotional connections between parents and their college-age children.

Our unique perspectives have helped inform our method. First of all, we are parents and both know the desire to be close to our children and maintain that connection. Second, we are both university professors and have spent years working with, advising, and counseling young adults just like your children. We have been at college our entire careers, teaching freshmen-level through graduate-level courses. We know students' struggles, and we've seen the difference a strong parental relationship can make in their lives. Finally, we are trained and licensed as family therapists. We are clinical faculty members who conduct family therapy and supervise family therapy just about every day. We know how to bring people closer together; as such, we are relationship experts. We know our subject matter very well. So, with this expertise and background, we believe we can help you strengthen the relationship you have with your college student. We encourage you to

Seven Letters

consider the possibility that strengthening the relationship between you and your child can be as simple as writing seven heartfelt letters.

The Current College Environment and What Your Child Needs from You

I t may have been years since you were a college student yourself, or maybe you never attended college. Either way, it's probably appropriate for us to provide a brief overview of your student's development within the current college environment and outline a balanced parenting approach in order to explain how writing these seven letters to your child could serve to build and strengthen your relationship.

The Current College Environment and Young Adult Development

A recent research project conducted with first-year students at a liberal arts college in the Midwest required students to journal about their freshman-year experience. A review of these journal entries revealed that students felt isolated, lonely, and disconnected from others on campus. In addition, students reported using alcohol in detrimental ways and being ashamed of their actions in this regard. In their journals they would vow not to use alcohol again in a similar manner, but subsequent entries, some even within the same week, would reveal that students were repeating negative and unhealthy patterns of alcohol use. Feelings of loneliness and disconnection as well as unhealthy drinking choices typified many of their first year experiences. This study alone should highlight the importance of having someone to turn to for guidance and direction.

> *A key task for this age group is to learn to successfully negotiate relationships.*

Arthur Chickering[1] pioneered a model of college student development, outlining seven different "vec-

1. Chickering, A. W. and Reisser, L. (1993). Education and identity. 2nd Ed. San Francisco: Jossey-Bass.

tors of development" that college students negotiate. Developing competence, managing emotions, moving through autonomy toward interdependence, and developing mature interpersonal relationships are the first four vectors he describes. The vectors following these include establishing identity, developing purpose, and developing integrity. Chickering's work dovetails nicely with the work of other human development researchers who stress that some of the key developmental tasks for college students are to establish a coherent identity and learn to successfully negotiate interpersonal relationships.

So, how is knowing this important to you? Good question. Moving from "being a child living at home" to "being an adult living on your own" is a path filled with both happiness and turmoil. We believe that when you realize that two of your child's major developmental tasks are to forge a unique adult identity and learn to successfully negotiate interpersonal relationships, you can better understand your child and his world.[2] It can help you make a real connection. More importantly, it can help you to be understanding when your child

---

2. For ease of reading and to avoid sexist language, we will alternate references to the child's gender throughout the book. Some chapters will refer to sons, others to daughters.

makes choices of which you don't approve, and it can help you to be a more effective parent when interacting with him around the consequences of these choices.

Two Types of Parenting

We have witnessed two extreme types of parenting in the families of the college students we've work with. We touched on one extreme earlier; this is the "helicopter parent." This moniker has been given to those parents who hover over their children to ensure that nothing detrimental happens during the school years. These parents (and sometimes their lawyers) are found in advising offices, Dean's offices, financial aid lines, etc., making sure their child is being taken care of and that every detail of their child's college experience proceeds as it should. They are ever ready to swoop down to assist their child when the going gets tough.

I (S.H.) recently had an experience with someone who might fall close to the "helicopter parent" end of the parenting continuum. I was contacted by a mother whose son had just completed his first semester at our university. His grades were poor, and he was put on academic probation. His mother sought me out for words of advice. Through the conversation I indicated that I thought her son might not be ready for college and that some time at home, away from the university environment, would be a good thing. She was concerned that pulling him out of school would set him back and destroy his confidence. She said, "If I take him out of school, won't he see that as a manifestation that I don't think he is doing well? Won't it shake his confidence?" I responded with, "He's not doing well and taking him out of school might be the wake-up call he needs to realize he cannot take this opportunity for granted." She struggled with this course of action. Eventually, she asked me, "Well, what would you do if he was your son?" I told her that if he were my son, he'd be at home for the next semester, and he would be working to pay me back for the tuition I had spent. She couldn't believe this and asked, "You would do that to your own son?" I responded with, "In a heartbeat!" I was a bit surprised that this parent was more concerned with her son's fragile sense of confidence, and with what his peers might think of him not being in school, than she was with seeing how she could use the situation as a valuable teaching moment. This desire to spare his feelings was overriding an opportunity to teach him a potentially life-changing lesson.

We believe the idea of the "helicopter parent" has been around for some time (the new millennium did not invent protective parenting) but societal conditions may have produced an upswing in them over the last couple of decades. It is possible that this parental attitude is merely the product of raising children in a fear-based society where we are led to believe that, around every corner, bad things can happen. Like us, these parents have raised their children in a world with safety restraints, safety glass, safety seats, and even safety pajamas (non-flammable sleepwear). Thanks, in part, to overactive imaginations, fueled by media attention to missing children on milk cartons, war on drugs, war on terror, pedophiles on every block, and predators on the internet, these parents would not allow their children to play outside without adult supervision. They knew the whereabouts of their children at all times. These children did not experience riding in the front seat of the car (until they were a certain height and weight) nor did they deal with the simultaneous joy and frustration of negotiating the transmission hump while making a bed on the floor or the back seat of the car. Those of us raised before all these safety measures are sometimes surprised we lived through childhood at all. We don't mean to disparage wise safety measures—we observe them ourselves with our own children. We just believe that the overall safety consciousness of our society has strongly influenced the creation of over-protective parents.

At the other parenting extreme, we have the "hands-off" parent. These are typically people who, for one reason or another, have very little to do with their child's educational experience. As university faculty members, we don't see many of these parents until graduation. They tend to let their children negotiate their college career with minimal input. Sometimes these parents are vehemently opposed to providing any kind of assistance because, as we have heard from them, "I didn't receive any help when I was going to college and I turned out OK!" Some even report being better off for not having received any help. These "hands-off" parents are often too involved with work, hobbies, the rearing of other children, or in some cases too distracted with their own lives to attend to the parent-child relationship once the child has gone to college.

Striking a Balance

It's difficult for us to imagine that children at college would want either an overinvolved parent or a hands-off parent to help them negotiate the struggles and celebrate the successes of college life. Our hope is that the strategy we introduce will encourage a balanced approach to parenting a college student. Aristotle wrote about achieving the "golden mean" in life, referencing the idea that too much of any one thing in life can be detrimental. We believe this golden mean can be effectively applied to parenting college-age students. Somewhere between hovering over and turning your back on your child, there exists a space of parenting, a middle ground that allows grown children to make decisions and to also be held accountable for them. That space should also allow children to see their parents as three-dimensional human beings. This space can be achieved when parents and children begin to develop an adult-to-adult relationship.

Parents influence their children and can still effectively teach them, even at a distance.

We believe that parents who can find the balance between the extremes would be available for their children when needed and would stay at a distance when the children need to negotiate a situation on their own. This parent would have to possess an understanding of the developmental tasks facing young adults and would have to be willing to work on an adult-to-adult relationship with their children as they grow and mature. This parent would acknowledge that their children are capable of making decisions and choices and that they need to be prepared to either reap the full benefits of these decisions or face the full consequences.

One example of such a parent comes to mind. One of our students turned in two consecutive semesters of straight Fs. When I (S.H.) asked her the reason for her poor performance, she simply indicated that she was spending some time with a friend, just watching a lot of television. No drugs, no extra job, no depression, no family drama at home causing a distraction—no other reason except that she just quit going to class because she liked watching TV. When her mother found out that she had paid tuition for two full semesters so her daughter could watch TV, she immediately wanted to know what her daughter's plans were to pay back the tuition money she had spent. The daughter spent the next four months working with her mother in a home cleaning service to pay back the tuition. She came back to school with an appreciation for what the degree could mean to her, and she turned her academic career around dramatically. As she worked alongside her mother, she also learned about the sacrifices her mother had been making so she could attend college. From a parenting perspective, however, the biggest lesson in this experience was that the student could still trust her mother to set reasonable limits and follow through with those limits. Both mother and daughter have begun to see each other from more of an adult-to-adult perspective since this encounter. Parents still have an influence in the lives of their children and can still effectively teach them, even at a distance.

We think the suggestions in this book can help parents and their children find this golden mean and begin to develop a relationship that acknowledges the changes that are taking place between them. While we won't promise any miracles, we believe connecting with your child in a new way still borders on the miraculous. At least it can feel that way.

How Parents and Adult Children Connect

A t birth, children are completely dependent on their parents and have very little say in decisions that touch their lives—what diapers they wear or what food they eat. Very quickly, however, most children begin to assert some independence and express their will. Sometimes, especially in the early years, this requires parents to provide structure and a safe environment to keep their children's curiosity and enthusiasm from endangering them physically or emotionally. By the time U.S. children hit the mid-elementary school years, most parents allow their children to be fairly independent, giving them control over picking out clothes, making friends, and deciding what to eat. The balance of decision-making shifts more toward children in early adolescence because parents want children to learn from the consequences that come from their good and bad choices. This new level of agency notwithstanding, most parents remain very involved in the lives of their children by giving advice, rewarding or punishing certain behaviors, and helping children balance the demands of school, home life, and friends.

> *The only power you really have is the power they give you.*

By the time most children reach late adolescence and are ready to enter college, however, parents must adjust to the reality that they only have limited influence in the lives of their children. In fact, we contend that the only power you really have in their lives by this age is the power they give you. If they still happen to listen to you, then they are doing it because they love you, because they respect your wisdom, or maybe because they don't want to disappoint you. In essence, they are giving you power to influence them and help them to continue to grow as they enter adulthood.

The Shift in Your Relationship

As children (and parents) get older, the nature of the parent-child relationship changes quite a bit. It changes from a hierarchical relationship where parents need to make a lot of decisions in order to protect their children and their children's future into a more balanced partnership. In this new partnership, parents and children have to negotiate with one another to plan and provide for the children's future. While this negotiation process is rarely easy or smooth, it seems to be an important part of individual development in Western culture. In reality, the near future—and sometimes the entire future—of your relationship with your adult children could hang in the balance at this important transition point.

In the U.S., one of the hallmarks of effective parenting is being able to successfully "launch" your children. This launching typically takes the form of your children being able to go off to college, the military, or to get a job and have their own apartment without being too much of a drag on family resources. But as much as we want our children to be independent and self-sufficient, we also hope that they would want to spend time with us. We desire a return on our years of hard work and sacrifice, and we want them to ask for our advice and tell us about their lives. We want to help them make decisions that will impact their future, and, most importantly, we want to matter to them.

This transition from teenager-to-adult is not made all at once, and it is not made easily. Not coincidentally, the change is also difficult for parents as they work to open up their relationship with their children and make it more balanced. While challenging, this transition is increasingly necessary for families to negotiate for a couple of reasons. First, with increasing life spans, parents and children are likely to live for many more years together with the real possibility of multigenerational homes and caregiving relationships. Second, given recent economic instability, it is not uncommon for families to experience a boomerang effect where children leave home for college or marriage but then need to return home for financial and emotional support.

In a perfect world, you will share your opinion only at opportune times, and you will guide your children only when they really need it, and you will say the right thing at the right time, every time. In this perfect world, you will help them believe in themselves, and they, as a result, will be confident in facing the challenges that you cannot face for them. Additionally, you will simultaneously balance your need for connection and their need for autonomy perfectly.

It's not easy being this good, but you have already done so many things perfectly, so this should be easy too, right?

OK, now back to reality—as with all parents, you have probably made some mistakes over the years: maybe you were too demanding on your child when you should have been more understanding, or maybe you were too easy on her when you should have forced her to try harder. Mothers and fathers make those kinds of mistakes because they are learning how to parent a teenager at the same time that their child is becoming one. And, as you know, this type of "on-the-job training" is not the easiest way to learn something so complicated. One of our clients once compared this complicated family process to overhauling an engine while the car is speeding down the highway at 80 miles per hour. This is a really good metaphor for describing the process, and we often refer to it when struggling to handle a situation with one of our own children.

Improving Your Connection

Despite the difficulties inherent in negotiating a shift in the parent-child relationship, and no matter how good or bad your relationship has been in the past, it has the potential to develop into a better one. Of course, the responsibility for this falls largely on you for three main reasons.

First, you are the parent, so you are the one who is expected to be patient and self-sacrificing, willing to put aside your needs for the good of your child. Later it will be your child's turn to be patient and understanding, but this doesn't usually happen until you are old and past the point of being able to gloat and really enjoy it.

Second, you are the leader in the relationship and the one who will model the new family roles by communicating that you are ready for a more balanced relationship. This is done in a myriad of ways, such as when you ask your child to weigh in on certain family matters, plan family activities around your child's school schedules and priorities, work together on the child's college budget, give your child the chance to solve her own problems, or exercise trust in your child to manage her own class schedule—including attendance. However, one of the most effective ways to show your child that you are willing to shift from a predominantly hierarchical to a more balanced relationship is to share your personal feelings and thoughts. This allows you to be more transparent and open about who you have been and who you are trying to be, which serves to invite your child to see you as a real person. This may be surpris-

> *He/she will learn as much about you as you already know about her/him.*

ing or even disorienting for her because she will discover that you don't always have the right answer, or that you have experienced loss or heartache in your life, or that you wish you had done some things differently. This will prove to be a good transition because she will begin to learn as much about you as you already know about her. For many parents and children, this can be very rewarding because parents shift their stance from "I am in charge of this relationship because you need my help" to "Together we are in charge of our relationship because we both love and care for each other."

Third, you are still a very significant person in your child's life. Your child still depends on you—financially for certain, but emotionally as well. Research findings suggest that college-age children are still influenced by their parents, even when they live away from home. One study reported by David Glenn in the *Chronicle of Higher Education* suggested that when parents tell their children not to drink alcohol, many actually listen and follow this advice.[1] While not all college-age children are going to comply with parental counsel, these findings suggest that

1. Glenn, D. (2005, August 22). When parents say "Don't Drink," student actually listen, scholar reports. *The Chronicle of Higher Education*. Retrieved from http://chronicle.com/article/When-Parents-Say-Dont/120986/.

parental reminders are heard by students and that their behavior can be influenced. Even though your child won't always show it, she will listen to you, and you can influence her life for good in many ways. So rest assured, you can make a difference, and you will probably be called upon over your child's college career to step in and help in many ways.

Ultimately, every parent worries about their child when she goes away to college. Parents wonder if their child is prepared for this huge life transition, and they worry about things like grades, eating habits, mental health, decisions about drinking or drug use, friends, choices about sex, ability to manage money, homesickness, and serious relationships. Our goal is not to stop you from worrying—we don't think we can, because worrying is just another manifestation that you care about your child. Instead, our goal is to help you develop a better, more connected relationship with your college student so that she will turn to you for help or advice and will also share her successes.

As therapists, we have discovered that the quickest and most sure way to enhance emotional connection is through open and honest self-disclosure. By opening yourself up to your child in in this new way, you can strengthen and enhance your relationship. In fact, something magical will happen when you and your child communicate with each other at this deeper level. We believe you have the power to strengthen your relationship with your adult child, regardless of how that relationship looks at the present moment—if you're estranged from your child, you can get closer; if you're already close, you can deepen that bond.

The Benefits of Letter Writing

Optimally, parents and their college-age children would have multiple opportunities to talk face-to-face about important topics. This is not always possible due to factors such as the geographic distance, the student's independence and desire for less parental interference, and (let's be honest) the parents' need to work more hours to help pay for college. However, with advances in communication technology, today's families have a variety of options for staying connected. In fact, it's commonplace for students to talk with Mom on their cell phone while walking to class, exchange instant messages with their brother when taking a study break, text

21

Dad during a boring lecture, and Facebook someone (or everyone) in the family throughout the day. This type of communication is convenient, quick, and easy to do while multitasking any number of other activities such as doing homework, watching TV, cooking, attending class, shopping, or socializing. Unfortunately, these technologies do a much better job with the *quantity* of parent-child communications than they do with the *quality*. In fact, these devices seem designed to allow us to connect with our children quickly but not deeply.

> *These devices allow us to connect with our children quickly but not deeply.*

Modern Communication

Texting, instant messaging, and Facebooking allow you and your child to exchange information easily; however, it is our belief that a dependence on these technologies may actually hinder the development of a close connection. The convenience of these technologies can lead one or both of you to communicate in short bursts, fitting these essential and potentially meaningful family conversations around less valuable matters instead of scheduling a specific time to talk in depth. While you can cover a lot of details and discuss plenty of ordinary topics using these tools, they are poorly designed to help you iron out disagreements, talk about bad news, or strengthen your relationship. Indeed, it is extremely difficult to ensure, at the moment you're ready to address something serious, that you are both equally focused on the conversation, emotionally available to one another, and in a non-distracting setting. In these situations, it is typical for the person who begins the phone call or text exchange to be thinking about the relationship and what needs to be said, but the person who responds may be busy with a job, homework, at a party, or in school. In fact, the very nature of these communication tools allows for multitasking, which can mean that a math problem, an attractive classmate, or the SUV merging into your child's lane will be battling for his attention at the same time that you are pouring out your heart. Come on, parents! For that moment when you really want to connect with your child about something meaningful, the medium you choose should demand his full attention. Email might be an appropriate medium to address matters of importance but our email messages are easily deleted or become collateral damage in an instant when a hard drive goes belly up.

Letter Writing: The Advantages for Our Day

While today's technology affords you several options for

saying what you want to say when you want to say it, we believe the best way to connect with your child is among the oldest—the written letter. Historically, letters have helped family members and loved ones feel less isolated and more connected during times of separation. As mentioned by James R. Bitter, a marriage and family counselor, "the written letter has long been used to achieve closeness and contact at a distance, . . . [and] letters serve as a bridge across physical and emotional distance" (p. 6)[1]. The remainder of this chapter will discuss the advantages of letters and will explain how they can help maintain, and even build, connections between you and your child. (If you are already sold on the idea of writing letters and just want some guidance on how to write them, feel free to skip to the next chapter.)

Personal letters are a rarity in today's electronic age. In a 2011 survey, the U.S. Postal Service found that the average American household only receives personal letters once every seven weeks (down from once every two weeks in 1987).[2] The number of personal letters received

---

1. Bitter, J. R. (2000). Letter for a change: Using letter writing in marriage and family counseling. In R. E. Watts (Ed.), *Techniques in marriage and family counseling (Vol. 2)*, pp. 5-11. Alexandria, VA: American Counseling Association.

2. Schmid, R. E. (2011, October 3). You never write any more; well, hardly anyone does. Associated Press. Retrieved from http://www.msnbc.msn.

by today's young adult may be even fewer. Curious about this possibility, we asked a class of 40 undergraduates to indicate if they had received a letter or card in the mail from someone in their family in the last year. Only six students raised their hands. We then

Any letter from home is going to be seen as unexpected and exciting.

asked these students to keep their hand raised if the mailing was from someone other than their grandma, which left only two people with their hands still raised. Where daily mail deliveries were anticipated in the past, they are now tolerated, or even dreaded, because the majority of what we receive is bills or junk mail. Consequently, any letter from home is going to be seen as unexpected and exciting. So when your college student sees an envelope with familiar handwriting and his home address, he will automatically be interested in the letter's contents and recognize it as something special.

There are more than just nostalgia-based advantages to letter writing, however. Letters interrupt the normal flow and chaos of your college student's life, shifting away from the environments wherein he usually communicates with others. This shift away from "the typical" helps

com/id/44760552/ns/technology_and_science-tech_and_gadgets/t/you-never-write-any-more-well-hardly-anyone-does/#.T-PdwMXF-So.

create a moment in time that is different from most of his previous life experiences. Letter writing and, more importantly, letter reading are not as likely to be prone to the distractions associated with multitasking. While distractions are impossible to eliminate, they are less likely to occur as you write your letter because you will be concentrating on what you are writing, thereby increasing the probability that the information in the letter will be well received. Similarly, letters (especially handwritten letters) present the reader with the opportunity to focus on your message as he works to read and understand it.

Another major advantage of writing letters is that they are very helpful for those who express themselves better in writing than by speaking. This can remove, or at least reduce, your anxiety about saying the wrong thing, simply because the letter writing process allows for multiple attempts to get it right. Also, as suggested by James R. Bitter, letter writing can be done in a calmer state than face-to-face conversations, which can be helpful when discussing heartfelt topics or hot-button issues. Parents can write certain things and then read them through the eyes of their child, making necessary corrections to the letter before it is sent.

Furthermore, written words are more permanent. While there are clear advantages to staying connected through electronic means, your child may approach the mountain of these communications like the rest of us and delete any heartfelt messages in order to make room for messages to follow. As a result, your tenderly spoken voicemail or carefully worded text may be simply deleted. Most people do not keep electronic communications—even email—in a keepsake box, diary, or journal. Writer Joseph M. Schuster suggested that, "We don't write letters any more. We dash off email and text messages. We send our love into the world as ephemeral electrons. It won't clutter our closets, and our children won't have to sort through it when we die. It's efficient, it's convenient, and it's fast. But in one click, it's gone."[3]

As a point of fact, we assure you that your child won't throw away your handwritten letters with the same disregard with which he may delete voicemail or email. After all, letters represent tangible evidence of the message enclosed, whether that message is associated with love or concern. Responding to the aforementioned decline in personal letters to U.S. households, Aaron Sachs, a professor of American Studies and History at Cornell University, noted, "We don't have the intimacy that we have when we go to the attic and read grandma's letters. Part

---

3. Schuster, J. M. (2006, February/March). The lost art of letter writing. *Mary Engelbreit's Home Companion* (2), 112.

of the reason I like being a historian is the sensory experience we have when dealing with old documents and letters."[4] Apply this to your situation and imagine your child going through the steps of: (1) opening the mailbox, (2) sorting the mail and finding a letter from you, (3) eagerly opening the envelope and unfolding the letter, and (4) reading your words, handwritten on paper, with a message that will make a difference for your relationship. As you picture this scene unfolding for your child, hopefully you can understand why the intentionality of letter writing is so important for both the writer and reader.

It Really Works

We know that students see the value in letters from home. An undergraduate student in one of our classes wrote the following: "One thing that my mother could do to help me feel closer to her would be to send me letters in the mail. She has sent a few . . . but only on holidays and special occasions. To have a written letter from her—sent 'just because'—would give me something tangible to have in my possession with words from her heart."

---

4. Schmid, R. E. (2011, October 3). You never write any more; well, hardly anyone does. Associated Press. Retrieved from http://www.msnbc.msn. com/id/44760552/ns/technology_and_science-tech_and_gadgets/t/you-never-write-any-more-well-hardly-anyone-does/#.T-PdwMXF-So.

Our own experiences confirm these words. For instance, I (R. B.) received a letter from my father while I was away at college more than 22 years ago. At the bottom of this letter in his neat handwriting, my father wrote a simple, but deep, answer to a dilemma I had shared with my parents the previous week. I had been dating my girlfriend (now my wife) for some time, and though we were talking about getting married, I was unsure how I would know I was ready to get married. In Dad's letter, he wrote, "Son, you asked if we had any more good advice. If you have met someone you want to share the rest of your life with, then marry her. If you have doubts, then wait."

I vividly remember that moment—I read and reread that line of advice off of a hard copy letter while sitting in my apartment at college. There was a tangible feel to the paper that added a specific sensory memory. Beyond just the realization that this was good advice, the letter also served as proof that although my parents had been thinking about me and were willing to help, they were also willing to trust me to make this all-important decision on my own. Those two implied messages—"We love you" and "We trust you"—were what I needed at the time to calm my general doubts about myself and my specific worries about marriage. I know my father doesn't remember sending this particular letter, but I sure remember receiving it, because it gave me an answer to a simple yes–no question, an answer for which I have been extremely grateful over the years. To this day, seeing, feeling, and rereading Dad's note to me takes me back to a moment in time that I'll always treasure.

This is another advantage to letters and notes—they can be read multiple times, which means that you will have several chances to get your message across. This creates a much larger opportunity for you to provide your child with ideas to reflect on and to integrate into his life. In many ways, an encouraging letter from parents can be seen as being an initial inoculation against despair, loneliness, or discouragement at the first reading; then, your student will place your letter in his desk drawer or backpack, where it waits as a booster shot against these same ailments when he rereads it. The bottom line: it's more than a letter—it's a piece of you. It represents a connection and your new presence in your child's life. It represents a moment frozen in time that can help bring you closer to your college student.

> *It's more than a letter—it's a piece of you.*

Some Burning Questions

Simply put, this book is designed to guide you through a letter-writing campaign to help you get closer and develop a more meaningful connection with your college-age student. However, a successful campaign will require a significant commitment on your part to dedicate the time necessary to creating a well-crafted letter. Many parents need a few questions answered before they are willing to make this commitment. With this in mind, we have answered some of the most common questions below.

> *What do I do if I am uncomfortable expressing myself in a letter or feel negatively about my writing abilities?*

Many people share this concern. The best advice we can give is to make a commitment to writing these letters. Write a couple of rough drafts, if you have to. Have someone you trust read the letters before you send them. As we've mentioned earlier, the art of communicating effectively is being lost. Those who want to change this trend in their homes will find that it doesn't come easily, but they will also find it is well worth the time and effort. Remember, the letters you write stand a good chance of becoming treasured keepsakes and family history documents. As such, they require some time, attention, and intentional effort to make them special.

How do I approach my child after sending these letters?

All parents who take on this project will eventually talk to their child after he has read one of the letters. The biggest thing you need to decide is if you want to address the issue or if you want to wait for him to bring it up. The answer to this question will depend on your child, and only you can know whether your child will prefer to have you to bring it up or to have you wait and let him lead. Be prepared to tell him why you've decided to reach out to him in this way—let him know how much he means to you and how much you'd like to connect on a more adult level. It is also fine to let him know that other letters are pending and that you'd be open to discussing the letters anytime he'd like.

> *This letter-writing campaign is about gently offering an invitation for connection.*

What do I do if a divorce or other family difficulty has negatively impacted my relationship with my child?

Throughout the book, we have tried very hard to use examples that show a range of family relationships. We are aware that divorce, death, abuse, or other unpleasant events may have played a role in shaping your family's relationships. This letter-writing campaign is about gently offering an invitation for connection, despite your foibles or shortcomings. It's about reconnecting and testing the waters to see if your child is ready to see their parent-child relationship move to a more adult-to-adult level. If you shoulder the majority of the burden for the end of your marriage, or some other family difficulty, this is a great chance to clear the air by addressing, in a new way, how much you'd like to have done things differently, how important your child is to you, and how you wish your relationship with your child were stronger (see Chapter 7 – The Hindsight is 20/20 Letter).

What do I do if the letters don't have the desired effect—if my child still is distant or is just confused?

This is where the old adage, "You can lead a horse to water but you can't make it drink" applies. This letter-writing process is *an invitation* to connect (or to reconnect in some cases). The letters are written from your experiences, thoughts, and feelings as the parent. There should never be a case where the letter is being used to call your child to repentance or to make him feel responsible for your feelings. A blaming tone is not congruent with the purpose of these letters. However, if your child reads the letters and chooses not to allow you into his life, there is not much you can do. Perhaps so much hurt has occurred that your child isn't going to forgive you after simply reading your letters. Still, we believe that your letters will not be discarded either physically or emotionally. Your letters are a part of you and are a gift to your child. Even if your letters do not produce dramatic changes immediately, we believe they may still represent the beginnings of a dialogue that will eventually develop.

My child and I are not even on speaking terms—
how can I know if my efforts will be worth it?

If you and your child are not speaking, we simply ask, "What have you got to lose?" There is a lot of research that suggests that the healing power of letters is not only for the reader but for the writer as well. Writing down your thoughts and reflections about important relationships can provide a venue for you to think about how you will do things differently if and when the opportunity arises. If it doesn't happen with your college student, perhaps you'll benefit by applying the lessons you learn from this experience to your other relationships.

What do I do if my spouse won't help in the letter writing?

There is no requirement that both parents should write the letters together. In fact, if the letters become something that comes from both Mom and Dad as a unit, it might actually lessen the uniqueness of each letter, as well as the overall purpose and impact of the exercise. There is a real benefit to having your child get to know you personally—not as a parent, but as another human being with strengths, weaknesses, fears, and hopes that are unique to you and separate from those of your spouse. So if you have a spouse who doesn't want to write, that's fine. However, as you embark on this journey be aware that your spouse will certainly want to know how it is going and will be very interested to see the changes in your relationship with your child.

What do I do if my child figures out I am writing these letters with the help of a book?

Let's face it—if you start writing these letters, out of the blue, and you begin to pour out your heart to your child in a way that he's never experienced before, he's going to know something is up. You will absolutely need to be prepared to answer the "Why is mom writing these letters?" question. If he figures out you're receiving assistance from a book written by two family therapists, simply let him know how much he means to you and that you wanted to make sure you got the help and support necessary to successfully undertake this connection process. In the new millennium, people are becoming more comfortable with not knowing all the answers, and we're hopeful that your act of engaging in this process with the help of our book will be an example that your children will follow when they have their own adult children.

How do I approach letter writing differently if my child is living at home or in my same city?

The principle of open self-disclosure at the foundation of this letter-writing campaign remains the same, regardless of the manner in which your child receives the letters. If you'd like, place the letters in his room or still send the letters by mail—it doesn't really matter. Sure, your child may think it is a bit strange to get a letter from Dad, delivered by mail to the same address, but this may even add to the uniqueness. With a child living at home or in the same city, you will still have the same experience as other parents who take on this exercise and will eventually need to have the conversation about why you've decided to reach out in this manner. Be prepared to share your reasons with your child.

The 4 Suitcase Letter

Arriving on campus can be an overwhelming experience. It is a time of firsts. Students are meeting new
roommates, negotiating new rules, sharing new
spaces (often with a bunch of strangers), and basically just
trying to keep their heads above water. Some students are
reluctant college attendees—they'd sooner be back at home
with their high school friends in familiar territory. Other
students seem to have been made for going away to college—they've been ready for the first week of college since
their first week of high school. Regardless of what type of
kid you have, the first week is typically a time of transition
and change. Depending on the individual, this transition

can be nerve-wracking, exciting, or a combination of the two. During times of transition, new students need permission to hold onto some things that are familiar as well as encouragement to venture out and brave the new world. A letter setting the tone for the first few weeks of your child's college experience can provide both of those things.

Purpose of the Suitcase Letter

The Suitcase Letter is intended to be a message from home that helps set the tone for your student's first weeks at school. With this in mind, the letter should send the message that school is an exciting time and that you have every confidence that your child will make the most out of the opportunities that will come her way. The letter must also acknowledge that the first weeks of school can be stressful. It's difficult to connect with your child if she doesn't feel as though you understand what she's experiencing. The successful letter will touch on three main elements: (a) your knowledge of her excitement or apprehension to be at school, (b) your knowledge about who she is and the characteristics she uniquely possesses, and (c) the confidence you have in her to be successful.

This is going to be the first letter that your child will

This letter might be a bit of a surprise for your child.

receive from you, so you are setting the stage for things to come. While this letter might be a bit of a surprise for your child, it probably won't be as surprising as the letters that follow. However, what might be surprising about this letter is the tone that it takes. After all, this is the first in a series of letters that will invite her to relate to you in a deeper, more personal way. We call it the "Suitcase Letter" because we want you to slip it into her bag before the two of you say goodbye to each other.[1] Hopefully, she will read the letter after you've dropped her off and will have some time alone to digest your words. For those of you whose child still lives at home, consider it "backpack" or "lunchbox" letter and place it accordingly.

Basic Elements to the Suitcase Letter

As you begin to think about writing this letter, you might consider the time when you first left home. What pearls of wisdom do you remember getting from your parents or other influential people? Was it a time of excitement or worry? Were you going into a situation where you had some social support networks already in place, or were

---

1. We also know that with all that is going on to get a child ready for school, you may not have the time to get it into the suitcase. So, don't let the title of this chapter deter your efforts to write this type of letter. Good luck!

41

you fully expecting to build these from the ground up? What things were you not told about that you wish you had known?

As with all of the letters we recommend in this book, we believe the most successful letters are going to be those that show the real you, that come from your heart, and that avoid preaching or lecturing. It is important to remember that even the most benign words of recommendation or advice may be met with resistance if you and your child are not on the same relational page. So, share your experiences, your innermost thoughts, and open up to your child.

For most young adults, this is the first time they won't have some kind of curfew or some requirement to check in with mom or dad. Of course, there are always the text messages that you'll exchange, but you won't be present to verify that they're tucked in bed nicely. Think about the first time you left home to be on your own—what do you remember about the realization that you didn't have people to account to anymore? What about when you realized that you didn't have someone to look after you the same way that mom and dad did?

For many, this is also going to be a time where expectations might not play out as intended. We've seen this happen a lot with best friends from high school who room together at college. Many quickly find out they can't stand being with each other 24/7; sometimes, the distance they had in high school was just enough of a break so that they could be best friends. Disappointments in expectations can also happen with their chosen major or even with the courses they have in their first semester. Don't be afraid to talk about your own expectations that never materialized. Talk about how you managed to make lemonade when life handed you lemons.

Make sure to talk about the hidden surprises, those people you met during your first month away that, at first glance, you thought were weird or different but turned out to become your lifelong friends. Or let her know that the chemistry course you were dreading turned out to be a game changer for you because it opened your eyes to new career paths or because that particular class is where you met the love of your life. It's all about possibilities, and your letter can be a big influence in letting your child know that there is much to experience at this time of life.

Kids love to hear stories from their parents' childhood. If your child knows her grandparents, she might want to hear about the advice you received from Grandma or Grandpa. This can offer an opportunity for you both to laugh about advice that now seems outdated or obsolete. If you do it right, you can tailor your story so that your child knows that whatever the content of the advice was, the real message you took away was that your parents loved you and wanted what was best for you.

By reading this book and considering writing these letters, you've indicated an interest in being a continued source of influence in your child's life. Trust us, if your Suitcase Letter avoids preaching and words of warning and comes from a place of open self-disclosure, your child will receive it as the invitation you want it to be.

Letter Starters

In this chapter and the ones that will follow, we include some key phrases that you can use to begin your letter. As you know, sometimes the hardest part about writing is just getting started. Take your time and review these letter starters and begin to share some of what you want to give your child at this important moment in her life and yours.

- *Before I left home, your grandfather tried to give me advice on how to act while I was away. I remember him trying to make it a serious occasion, but _____.*

- *I remember being so nervous when I left home. The weeks leading up to my departure seemed to fly by, and I remember thinking, "I'm not ready yet . . . there is so much to do." Eventually, _____.*

- *I just wanted to drop you a note to let you know how excited I am for what lies ahead of you. Though you've been in our home for 18 years, it seems like only yesterday that _____. (Fill in the blank with a memory you have that she might not remember.)*

- *There was a time when you and I _____. (Fill in the blank with a shared memory and what you keep in your heart about that moment.) That memory will stay with me forever, even though you'll be miles away. I know that _____.*

- *I know you're feeling swamped right now and that there is so much on the line. You've always bring your best effort to any situation—even when the odds are against you. Do you remember that time in soccer when _____.*

- *I'm so excited for you. College was made for people like you. I can totally see you making tons of new friends. When it comes to friendships you _____.*

- *I want you to know that even though we'll be missing you, we know you are doing the thing you've always dreamed of doing. And about*

> *that dream, don't worry too much if it doesn't seem to materialize immediately. It always takes a little time to get in the groove. I remember when you started kindergarten _____.*

Excerpts from Suitcase Letters[2]

I have a picture of you back at my office that I don't think you've ever seen. You must have been about three years old when it was taken. I look young—I had hair back then. Honestly, I don't need to look at the actual picture that often because the moment is truly frozen in my mind. We must have been tickling each other or wrestling because you are laughing, and you look so happy. I've always appreciated that you have a cheery nature about you.

There are so many other happy moments that I carry around in my heart and mind. Over the last couple of months I've been looking at that picture and can't believe that the time has gone by so quickly. Hard to believe

---

2. To avoid sending the message that there is a specific type of letter, or a "right way" to write these letters, we are only providing excerpts from hypothetical letters throughout the book (as opposed to full letters). This will help ensure that the letters come from you and not some predetermined letter template. We hope the excerpts convey a range of ways to write these letters, that you'll see a bit of what you would write to your own child, but also that these excerpts will inspire you to write your own letter - the one that you need to write and the one that your child needs to read.

you're at school and living on your own. Despite my best efforts to make time stand still, you grew up.

* * *

When I left home, I remember getting all kinds of advice about how to act, what to do in certain situations, and to remember who I was. That last one always made me laugh. "Remember who you are." I think my dad thought I was prone to amnesia or something.

I don't know that I always followed the advice I was given, but, looking back, I know that when I did receive advice, it came from a place of love and caring. Even when Dad and I were at odds with each other, I knew he loved me. He was never going to be the kind of guy who would open his heart and pour out emotions, which actually bugged me when I was younger—I wanted him to be more open. But looking back now, I know he did love me and wanted what was best for me. I remember him making sacrifices for us, small ones here and there, like not having dessert so we could or going without new clothes so that we could have them. It wasn't until much later that I found out he had taken a second job when I went to school so Mom could stay at home with the younger kids, and they wouldn't have to take a loan to pay for my college tuition. Mom only recently told me about that. I wish I had known that when he was alive. I would have been more appreciative for the things he did and would have told him so.

* * *

I know it that this first month is going to be a transition for you. It might even be a bit stressful. For me, nothing I did in high school prepared me for the pace of college—even college-prep English. All we did was diagram sentences, and I don't think I ever did that in college. I was expected to know how to write, and I never learned in high school that writing is simply thinking on paper. It took me a long time to get that down. Maybe it's the kind of thing that takes a whole lifetime to learn to do well. But the pace of college was such a shock to me. In high school it seemed like we took two weeks to study one chapter of psychology. In college it's more like a chapter a day. I think it took me getting a couple of Ds on my first tests to realize I needed to step it up or I wasn't going to make it.

* * *

I really hope that I didn't hide this letter so well that you never see it. I just wanted to share a couple things with you. You know that I never got to go to college. I was a young adult at a time when a college education wasn't as necessary as it is now. When I look around at work, I see all of my college-educated colleagues, and I must admit that I have two reactions: I'm proud of what I have become in my profession despite not having had a formal education, and I'm sad that I never got to do the things that so many college students get to do on a daily basis. Who knows? Maybe someday I'll go back to school and get my degree. I'll bet that would be a sight. The student newspaper headline could read, "Bald Guy Sitting Next To You Is a Student, Not a Nark."

I'm so excited to hear what your experience is going to be like. You have so much to offer, and you've always been inquisitive. I'm sure that there will be ups and downs, but I know you've always been the kind of person to rise above any struggles and make the most of the opportunities that come your way.

If this letter is thoughtful and comes from the heart, it will be a big hit. Don't be too surprised if you get a phone call immediately after your child reads it; but, by the same token, don't be too upset if you don't get an immediate reaction. Kids are all different in how they respond to parents. If your child begins to see you in a different light after reading your letter, you've successfully set the stage for the letters that will come. You'll also be well on your way to redefining how the two of you relate. Best of luck with the "Suitcase Letter."

5
The Praise Letter

O ver the past 60 years, scholars, specialists, the media, and other so-called "experts" have failed to reach consensus on the relative value of many popular parenting strategies. So it should come as no surprise that there are debates about the value of many parenting interventions such as spanking, grounding, natural consequences, treating your children like little adults, or paying for good grades. However, child development specialists agree that, regardless of the type of limits you place on your children or the philosophy that guides your parenting, children always benefit from sincere praise. In fact, praise is regularly recommended as one of the best ways for a parent to reinforce desirable behaviors, and it serves to strengthen the parent's relationship with their child, regardless of age. Praise is even well received by teens and college-age children—though they may appear to be unaffected by anything positive that others say to them.

Purpose of the Praise Letter

This chapter is designed to help you write a letter of praise to your child. Properly written, this letter will help him see his strengths and accomplishments as very real and very valuable. This letter is especially relevant for today's college-age students, who have grown up in an environment that is often

> *Children always benefit from sincere praise.*

full of deliberately harsh and unconstructive criticism. Civility in high schools is at an all-time low; hundreds of thousands of children in public schools report being bullied and exposed to a host of negativity on a daily basis. Many of these attacks come in subtle forms. For example, your child might post an innocent picture on Facebook, only to find that so-called "friends" have posted humorous, yet negative, comments about his clothing or physical appearance. This then works to undermine his emotional safety and causes him to second-guess his decision to share that part of his world with others. While you may have tried your best to shield your child from negativity, the relative ease of personal online attacks and the anonymity afforded in some electronic communications have led to an increase in the sheer volume of negativity that kids are exposed to, compared to kids thirty years ago. Receiving a letter of praise from you can contribute to your child's positive self-image and, in turn, help buffer him from an increasingly uncivil society.

A second factor that supports the need for this letter is that today's world is not very understanding of the basic traits that are so essential to healthy relationships and productive lives such as integrity, kindness, sensitivity, and courage. Our children experience a nearly constant media exposure, which can be a formidable challenge to maintaining a meaningful self-image, discouraging them and leaving them focused on the importance of temporary and superficial characteristics of appearance (body shape, skin complexion) or possessions (clothing, cars, electronics). In our increasingly celebrity-driven culture, children may be susceptible to the idea that true fulfillment comes from being famous, rich, or beautiful. Consequently, it is important to remind your child of his amazing and admirable *internal* qualities, characteristics, and successes.

Basic Elements to the Praise Letter

A thoughtful letter of praise can remind your child of his value and can be a buffer against the critical and sometimes unfeeling world of judgmental roommates, tough professors, and insecure dating partners. Included here are a few important guidelines to consider as you write this letter—a letter that can mean a great deal to both of you.

We also want to remind you that if you're following the book's suggested order, this will be the first letter that will arrive in the mail, so this will be a crucial step in the process of strengthening your relationship with your child, setting the tone for other letters that follow.

One of the first things you need to remember when writing this letter is that although your child is not perfect (you already knew that), there are certainly a number of characteristics he possesses that are praiseworthy. Focus on these attributes! Share your appreciation for these qualities, which may not be valued or even noticed by a superficial world. For example, in a culture that celebrates reality-TV drama queens, your child may be steady and easygoing, with relatively few emotional meltdowns. He may be a great listener or a loyal friend or someone who helps others feel important. These are not qualities that are going to be tested on a midterm exam or highlighted on live TV, so your child may need a reminder that these traits are unique, that they matter to you, and that you believe they will matter to others.

It may be helpful to consider how others—particularly friends—see him, as this may prompt you to consider how something that annoys you may be endearing to, or even valued by, other important people in his life. For example, if he spent a lot of time with friends in high school, you can remind him of his dedication to friends and his willingness to listen to other people's problems. If he is obsessed with music or social media or even video games, you can praise him for being devoted to something that will help him connect to his peers. Even if you don't fully approve of the time he spends on these activities, you can still talk about them in a positive manner; after all, they are much more positive than some of the other things that a college freshman can find to do around campus.

Recognize that many qualities, while bothersome or problematic in one setting, can actually be desirable in another. For example, the strong-willed, rebellious, authority-challenging high schooler can often turn into the independent-minded college student leader who doesn't follow the rest of the student body. Perhaps these qualities become key factors in his lifelong devotion to championing the cause of the little guy.

The big struggles will turn out to be pivotal moments where the two of you grew.

Furthermore, provide as much specific detail as possible in your letter of praise. This can take the form of short stories from his life that can remind him about his praiseworthy characteristics. Detailed accounts from your child's life will help you emphasize your points. It's always good for parents to remember positive moments in their children's lives. The act of writing these moments down will cement them into your memory and will help to balance out the less positive moments when your child made mistakes or you felt like disowning him.

In some cases, this may be a difficult letter to write if you have experienced some disappointments in your child or if he has made some mistakes after disregarding your good counsel. As much as possible, put his mistakes and obvious need for improvement aside and focus on the attributes that he does have. It can be helpful to consider the context of your child's life and how far he has come in dealing with his past shortcomings and current limitations. Perhaps the big struggles of the past will turn out to be pivotal moments where the two of you grew in your relationship by being forced to relate to one another in a different way. A letter of praise in this situation could emphasize how pleased you were that he hung in there with you during a particularly tough time and that you've been impressed with his resolve and dedication despite the unpleasantness of the whole situation.

Consider a scenario where your child might be struggling academically and not getting the grades that he is capable of getting. He has made some mistakes—you don't have to be in denial about that to write this letter. However, you can emphasize the positive even in the midst of the negative. More specifically, if he has done poorly on homework or tests,

- *but there are some extenuating circumstances such as illness or financial problems that can be considered, he can be praised;*
- *but he is learning from his mistakes, he can be praised;*
- *but he is still working hard, despite having a learning disability, he can be praised;*
- *but he came from a high school that did not prepare him well for college-level studies, he can be praised;*

- *but he is one of the first in the family to attend college, he can be praised.*

If you struggle to write this letter and worry that you may be too focused on your child's negative aspects, you might consider interviewing other family members or friends that love him and finding out what it is that they admire about him. This can be helpful in exposing you to other perspectives and in teaching you about the traits you rarely get to see in your child. For instance, many children can be irresponsible or disrespectful at home, but may be dependable, cooperative, and reliable at work or other settings. Both of us have reluctantly attended a parent-teacher meeting, expecting to hear that our kid was disrespectful in class, only to find out that the teacher believed our kids were model citizens and a delight to have in class.

Be careful not to give backhanded compliments, where you write something positive about your child followed by a negative. For example, "I am so proud of how much work you are putting into school," is praise, but "I am so proud of how much work you are putting into school; I am glad to see you finally living up to your potential" is demoralizing. This contains just enough of a jab that most children will not feel the original intent of the praise because they will feel deflated when their efforts are diminished.

Finally, as an extra safeguard, we encourage you to review what you have written before sending your letter. Have others read your letter if you are even a little worried about how your child might receive it on the other end. Remember that the intent of the Letter of Praise is to invite connection by sharing those things that you're most pleased about in him. He has plenty of voices that remind him about his mistakes or that communicate that he doesn't measure up to some standard. Your goal is to open a door for connection, to share both your admiration and your love.

Letter Starters

- *Ever since you were young, I have appreciated your ability to _____.*
- *Over the years, relatives, friends and neighbors have commented on a number of your great qualities, including _____.*
- *One of the best examples of _____ (fill in the blank with a quality you value in your child) is the time when you _____.*
- *I know that others have looked up to you because of _____.*
- *I am so proud of you for _____.*

- *Now that your sister is following you in high school, she is constantly reminded about the example you set. Not a day goes by without one of her teachers mentioning your _____.*

Excerpts from Praise Letters

I have been so impressed with how quickly you have made good friends since the move to college. I guess I should have seen this coming, based on our move from Texas the summer before your ninth-grade year. It is never easy to move, but it is especially difficult during high school, and I was so proud of you for making good friends and for working so hard to get past your shyness and your worry about being the new kid at school.

I have always thought of you as a good friend to others because you are so loyal—you don't talk about your friends behind their back. Also, it seems that when your friends are with you, it is impossible for them to feel down or discouraged because you lift them up with your energy and loving concern. I have seen this so clearly in the way you manage your friends and help everyone have a good time when you are all together.

* * *

I want to tell you that I appreciate how responsible you

are in taking care of your schoolwork and part-time job. You do a lot, and I appreciate it because I know that there are many of your classmates on campus who don't care as much as you do about working hard. Over the years, you have been helpful on many, many occasions—even when it wasn't convenient for you. You have always done a good job, and your mom and I appreciate the example of responsibility and hard work that you set for your brother and sister. This responsible nature has been obvious to others, as you were one of the first of your friends to get babysitting jobs, and you have been given some pretty big assignments at work over the years, especially during your senior year.

* * *

I know it isn't easy to be away from home—it can be really hard sometimes. But you seem to be so much more confident and at ease with yourself than I was when I was a freshman. I am really proud of you for all the friends you have made and how easily you have fit into things socially and emotionally. I think that part of this is because you don't take yourself too seriously and you invite friendly teasing from others. You make me laugh all the time, and I really do enjoy the times that you are willing to put up with me as your dad. In fact, I am smiling as I write this because I am so proud to be your dad. I love you very much and want the best for you. Thank you for helping me to be a better father and a better man.

* * *

You have a lot of great qualities, but let me mention just a few that have really stood out to me over the last few months. I appreciate how smart you are because it shows in your schoolwork, in your sense of humor, and in your ability to pick up on things in social situations. You have been blessed with a great combination of book smarts and people smarts, and this will be a great asset to you both now and in the future. People that have both of these are rare, so I know that you are special in this regard. No doubt, you are being prepared to be the kind of person and kind of friend who helps others make the most of their lives. It makes me proud to see you making good choices, some big and some small. I am so proud of you for being willing to speak up for yourself and ask tough questions. You really are a leader, but you do it in a way that is inviting to others. This shows a willingness to help others who are less fortunate than you. You have such a nice balance of internal strength and independence, and yet you are very humble and teachable.

Obviously, you're not always going to like everything about your child, and not everything he does is praise-worthy. He can cause you to feel angry and frustrated, but even at the height of these emotions, your dedication and love for him remains constant. Remember, the Letter of

It's a letter that you need to write—and he needs to read.

Praise needs to be sincere—you cannot fabricate praise for your child and still have him believe your words. Your child doesn't need you to like everything about him or support everything that he has done, but he does need to know that you like *some* things about him and that you are able to compliment him with genuine praise. Whether this is an easy or a difficult letter for you to write, it's a letter that you *need to write*—and he needs to read. We know your letter can become something meaningful to both you and your child.

The Family Legacy Letter

By the time this third letter arrives, your child will know that receiving a personal letter from Mom or Dad is something to be anticipated, and her curiosity will be piqued. At this point, your child's reaction will likely be the best way to measure the impact of your letters. For example, she could call you after reading your letters with a tearful voice, filled with emotional expressions of love and gratitude. If this happens—congratulations! We recommend that you treasure this moment and share it with others, as partial payment for a lifetime of sacrifice and at least a semester's worth of tuition. Second, she could call you, concerned that you have some life-threatening disease that is making you express things heretofore unsaid in your relationship. If this happens, it is also a moment that should be prized because it proves you are not as predictable as she thinks and demonstrates that you really do have a lot of power and influence in her life. Third, she could call questioning your sanity—jokingly or seriously—and could even inquire about the reasons for your letters. Finally, is the absence of a response, a stunned silence or awkward communication. While this might occur because she feels like she doesn't know who you are anymore, it is more likely that she just doesn't know what to say. The letters are probably making a difference in her life and are shifting how she thinks about you as a parent. Regardless of the response you get, *keep writing*. The process of thinking about your child and what you want to include in your next letter will keep you connected to her, despite the distance that may separate you.

For the purposes of this third letter, we want your focus to be on what your child stands to inherit from you, not in terms of money or property, but in terms of a family legacy. A number of authors and leaders have commented on the idea of family or individual legacies, and we have included a few powerful reminders for your review:

- *Thomas Scott, political activist and adventurer, wrote, "A man cannot leave a better legacy to the world than a well-educated family.[1]"*

- *William James, philosopher and psychologist, noted that, "The greatest use of life is to spend it for something that will outlast it.[2]"*

- *Abraham Lincoln, U.S. President, said, "I want it said of me by those who knew me best, that I always plucked a thistle and planted a flower where I thought a flower would grow[3]."*

- *W. E. B. Du Bois, famed African-American activist and author, wrote, "To increase abiding satisfaction for the mass of our people, and for all people, someone must sacrifice something of his own happiness. This is a duty only to those who recognize it as a duty. . . . It is silly to tell intelligent human beings: Be good and you will*

1. Scott, T. (2005). In Louis Klopsch (Ed.), *Many Thoughts of Many Minds: A Treasury of Quotations from the Literature of Every Land and Every Age*. Retrieved from http://www.gutenberg.org/dirs/1/7/1/1/17112/17112.txt.
2. James, W. 2005 [1880]. *Great Men and Their Environment*. Kila, MT: Kessinger Publishing.
3. Lincoln, A.(2006). Quoted in Steven Fantina (Ed.), *Of Thee I Speak: A Collection of Patriotic Quotes, Essays, and Speeches* (p. 90). Phillipsburg, NJ: Integritous Press.

be happy. The truth is today, be good, be decent, be honorable and self-sacrificing and you will not always be happy. You will often be desperately unhappy. You may even be crucified, dead and buried, and the third day you will be just as dead as the first. But with the death of your happiness may easily come increased happiness and satisfaction and fulfillment for other people—strangers, unborn babes, uncreated worlds.[4]"

In all the quotes presented here, authors speak of greater goals than just survival and of a higher purpose than just feeding and clothing oneself. The ideals they captured transcend the daily routines and demands of life, emphasizing certain values and actions that inspire others and give life greater meaning. For our purposes in this chapter, we define "family legacy" as the collective set of values held by family members and the corresponding actions that support these values. In this regard, a family legacy is everything that we say when describing our family, coupled with the stories that add substance and detail to our descriptions. In some instances, a family's

---

4. Du Bois, W. E. B. (2002). Commencement Address to Howard University. In Eugene F. Provenzo (Ed.), *Du Bois on Education* (Chap. 14, p. 196). Retrieved from http://books.google.com/books (Original speech given 1930).

legacy is communicated in deeds and accomplishments alone since there is truth to the adage that actions speak louder than words. However, most of the time, we communicate our family legacies to each other in the form of stories, passed down through generations.

Purpose of the Family Legacy Letter

The purpose of this chapter is to help you draw on your family legacy—the good and the bad—to pass along some life lessons to your child. After all, it is just as important for your child to know where she is from as it is for her to

Family stories allow parents to influence their child through indirect, although effective, means.

know where she is heading. Family legacies are powerful factors in determining our lives, and it is helpful to address your family's function and dysfunction with your child as she continues to mature. In fact, having these adult-type conversations with your child where you talk about her family is one of the best ways to communicate to her that you trust her and that you have noticed her maturity. Additionally, the proper use of stories about what other family members have done (or have not done) allows parents to influence their child through indirect, although effective, means.

Seven Letters

Before proceeding, let us say a little more about using family stories as an indirect approach in parenting, as it is especially important to consider when relating to your child at this developmental stage. Clearly, you can't parent the same way you did when your child was younger, and you can't nag, badger, or control her without some serious consequences in terms of relationship quality. In fact, given that personal autonomy is highly valued in our strongly individualistic U.S. culture, it's possible that your child may not appreciate your advice because she doesn't want to think of herself as needing your advice. If this is the case, even if you are giving the best advice ever, she may feel the need to demonstrate her independence by showing you that she is old enough to make her own decisions. While some young adults do respond to direct counsel, many in this age group resist being told what to do, especially if it is something that they already know they should be doing.

Our partial solution to this challenging relational dynamic is to use real-life examples from your family's recent or distant history. In this manner, you can inspire your child with a story of Grandma's tenacity or Uncle Billy's regrets—without having to point any fingers at your child directly. In doing so, you allow the written account of her ancestors to be the messenger as your letter communicates a message that can motivate or warn her without priming her to be defensive or avoidant. The Family Legacy Letter can also inspire her as it outlines what it means to be a member of your family, what your family stands for, and how generations of family members have all contributed to your family's identity. This can be a powerful letter, since stories of courage, sacrifice, self-sufficiency, service, and honor can be found in every family.

Basic Elements of the Family Legacy Letter

In preparation for this letter, you will want to do one or more of the following: (a) write down a list of things that your child has inherited from you and other family members; (b) ponder the characteristics and traits that have been demonstrated to her by extended family; (c) check any recorded family history or personal journals and note the examples found in the lives of her ancestors; and/or (d) talk to other family members to get at the core of what it means to be from your family. Using the information you have collected, you can write your child a letter that is both informative and inspirational. In it, you can tell her more about the family, and you can provide encouragement and character lessons based on the stories. It is important to realize that a letter written about your family legacy can send a strong message about your child's potential without saying things such as, "I want you to know what I expect from you" or "You've got some mighty big shoes to fill." If done well, your child will get the message and there won't be any preaching or lecturing necessary. This is simply a letter from you about your perspective of your family, your experience as a member of it, and what you've learned about what it means to be a Smith, a Martinez, or a Chang.

Letter Starters

- *When I think about the people that came before us, I think of your grandfather Baldwin, who was a great example of hard work. One of the best stories I have heard about this is when he _____.*

- *We don't know a lot about where our family comes from, but we believe some of them came to America because they desired to be free and to choose their own way. Along the way, they had to stand up for what they believed in, even when it was really unpopular. One example of this from our family history is the time that your great-, great-grandmother _____.*

- *Not every family is perfect and there have been*

lots of mistakes made in ours. One thing that we can all learn from is the example of your uncle, now serving prison time, who lost his way when he started drinking and got into trouble with the law. Because of him, the rest of us have worked harder to take care of the family name by doing things like _____.

- *Being a Washington means the following: being patriotic, taking care of the underprivileged, working hard, and playing hard. I would like to share a few stories about each of these qualities so that you know a little more about your ancestors and why our family legacy is so important to me.*

- *One of the best people that I ever knew was your grandma Jessie, and I am hoping that you can get to know her a little better as you read this letter. She was strong in many areas of her life, but she also had a fatal flaw—stubbornness. I hate to admit it, but I've got a lot of that stubbornness in me. There was this one time when she _____.*

This may be a difficult letter to write if you believe you have some rotten apples on your family tree or skeletons in your family closet. If this is the case, and you have some real tragedies, abuse, or dysfunction in your family's past, you have several options when deciding what to share. Your first option is to not say anything and take the family secret to the grave. Second, you can wait and talk about it with your child when you are face-to-face with her when she is not in the middle of a busy semester. Third, you can present the information to her (especially if she already knows something about it) in such a way that she realizes that mistakes were made in the family's past and that those mistakes don't ever have to be made again. Fourth, share the details so that your child sees the object lesson in what has happened.

As a final caution, be particularly sensitive when sharing any story about a family member or friend that might cause your child to lose that person as a role model. If and when you choose to share these particular types of stories, be sure to do so in person so that you can gauge your child's reaction to any surprising or disappointing news about someone that she has admired. Ultimately, even if you choose to avoid writing about serious family tragedies, still write *something* about your family because, in any family, there are always some important life lessons that need to be passed along.

Excerpts from Family Legacy Letters

When I was growing up I was always told that I was "just like Grandpa Wheatley." But as a kid I failed to see how the old man who moved around with the aid of a walker was anything like me. Recently, however, I've been looking through scrapbooks that my grandma handed down to my mom. I saw all these pictures of Grandpa when he was younger—I never knew he was a minor league baseball player or that he was a coal miner. By the time I knew him, he had left that part of his life behind, and he was newly retired from a career as a salesman for the office supply store.

As I looked through the pictures, I was blown away. There were pictures of him surrounded by his coworkers in the coal mine, showing him on his back with his pick ax at work, others of him asleep, obviously worn out by the day's work, and a group of pictures showing him with his buddies enjoying a beer and laughing. In other pictures (the baseball ones) he was always standing or sitting beside a Black man, the only Black man on his team. When I talked to my grandma about the pictures, she told me about how Grandpa and Ray (short for Raymond), were the best of friends. It was a friendship that many frowned upon, and your great-grandfather caught a lot of flak for hanging out with him. But he never understood why people thought the way they did about Ray. "To your grandpa," she said, "Ray was his best friend. They had a lot in common—they both loved baseball, both were dedicated husbands and fathers, and both had a love for their children."

I've seen glimpses of my grandpa in you as well. You've always seemed to accept others for who they are, and you have always looked out for them. You've always had a sense of what was "fair" or "right." I think this is part of our family legacy—the ability to reach out to others when no one else will, to think of others as fellow travelers, not as different people from different towns or the other side of the tracks. It makes me proud to be a Wheatley.

* * *

In sharing a few thoughts with you about my family's legacy, I feel a little nervous and worried. Worried because it is kind of like "putting lipstick on a pig" when I try to make us seem a little better than we actually are. And while I wish there was more of the good to talk about in our family, I want share with you a few things so you know what to watch out for.

On my side of the family, there is a pretty big problem with alcoholism. You know a lot about this because you have seen how the family has been negatively affected by

Grandpa's drinking and all the partying that my siblings have done. You have even seen some of what it has done to our immediate family with me and your dad. I just want to tell you a few things now so that you will know that this is something that you have to be careful about and is something that you can change if you want to.

In my family, we worked hard, and we played really, really, really hard. Almost every party or celebration started with a toast and included lots of drinking. In some ways, it helped us unwind and deal with the stress of life, but it almost always made things worse when people got hurt, arrested, or lost jobs. It has even ruined some family relationships. Those of us who have done the best have found other ways to unwind and de-stress. In fact, if you look at your dad now or your aunt Courtney, you can see some really good examples of managing stress and avoiding alcohol by replacing it with running, music, or coaching sports.

* * *

In many ways we are a forgettable family—just a typical middle-class family, like millions of other ones. We never had much, though we always have managed to save enough money to take you kids on a vacation, even if it was just camping. Someday you're going to stay in a really

77

posh hotel and realize all that you were missing out on by being born into our family. I secretly worry that when you do, you'll resent what little your father and I actually were able to provide. However, it still amazes me at what your dad was able to accomplish with only a high school education. Toward the end of his career, he was surrounded by young bucks each with an MBA in hand. He always felt outgunned in those meetings, but he held his ground and was welcomed at the table because of his integrity. No one looked down their nose at him because he was such a trusted commodity at the company. His bosses would come to him with business-related dilemmas all the time, but they would also come to him when they needed advice on how to raise a teenager, what to say at a daughter's wedding, or how to improve their marriage. We come from a long line of worker bees—not a queen bee amongst us—but we stand out because of our integrity and our work ethic. For years it has served your father well, and it continues to serve us well as a family. It has never made us rich, but we've never wanted for food or shelter.

You are the first of anyone in our family to go to college. Now it is your turn to take the family legacy and build on the rich tradition you've been handed. I can't wait to see what you make of the opportunities that lie ahead.

Using your family legacy as a basis for this letter will help your child better understand her roots. Properly understood, your heritage can inspire and give direction to a young adult struggling to figure out who she is and where she is going. Share the good and bad lessons learned from past or even current generations, and your child will be better positioned to face the challenges that freshman year (and beyond) will present her.

The Hindsight Is 20/20 Letter

In golf, a "mulligan" represents an agreement between golfers that someone can hit a second shot without a penalty—a "do-over"—if the first shot was totally off the mark. Taking a mulligan can get someone's game back on track; it is a gesture of good will from the other players that says, in essence, "This is only a game. What's important is that we're together playing, and let's move past that horrible shot." In life, we get multiple opportunities to take a mulligan with our children. Sometimes our do-overs happen when we have a second child and we just don't get as hung up with some of the battles we undertook as first-time parents. Other do-overs occur when we admit that a choice we made or line-in-the-sand that we drew was probably not the best approach to a certain situation. Luckily, most family members tend to be forgiving—maybe because they know that it is only a matter of time before they, too, will want the same courtesy from us.

Purpose of the Hindsight Is 20/20 Letter

The purpose of this letter is like taking a parenting mulligan. It provides an opportunity for you to reach out to a now-adult child and take responsibility for a past action that seemed important at the time, but in retrospect seems to have caused more

In life, we get multiple opportunities to take a mulligan with our children.

harm than good. Examples of this might be the time when you, in a state of anger, lashed out at your son and told him he could go live somewhere else; when you demanded that your child attend a certain school when he wanted to go to where his friends were going; when you accepted a job without deeply considering the impact the resulting move would have on your child; or, perhaps, when you should have taken a harder stance with your son because your actions failed to protect him from heartache and pain.

We, as family therapists, use terms such as "relational traumas" or "attachment injuries" to describe times when individuals do things to one another, whether intentionally or unintentionally, that damage their relationship. All such actions tend to compromise people's ability to really connect with one another, unless some resolution is made. This letter can help begin a process of getting things back on track. Even if the conflicts with your child were not traumatic or hurtful to you, if left unresolved, they can continue to be a wedge placed between you and your child.

The goal of this letter is simply to open a dialogue with your child, not to resolve any and all conflicts you may have experienced—that is asking way too much from a single letter. The important thing to do with this letter is to pick a single event that stands out to you as something that was either left unresolved or wasn't resolved to your mutual satisfaction and show your child that you are open to looking at it in a different, more healthy way.

If you are writing these letters in the order we suggest, this letter will be coming to your child at a time when he senses that you are trying to do something specific with your relationship through letter writing. Therefore, he might be more open to hearing you out than he has in the past. He will already be used to this letter format and, perhaps, may have begun talking with you in a different way as a result of the work you've done to this point.

Basic Elements of the Hindsight Is 20/20 Letter

The Hindsight Is 20/20 Letter can be a tricky letter to write. After all, once a negative situation has occurred and you've both seemed to move past it, the last thing you are inclined to do is to tempt fate by discussing it again. This letter should be written

You need to come at this process humbly.

in such a manner that there is no question in your child's mind that you are making a good-will gesture. At times when two people are working through a forgiveness process there can be a tendency for one person to feel either blamed or obligated to forgive the other person. This letter cannot be a letter of blame nor can it suggest that you both played a part in the conflict. Veiled or insincere attempts at apologies or reconciliation can sometimes sound like this: "Let's both admit that we could have done things differently" or "You've got to admit I wouldn't have acted the way I did if it wasn't for what you did." While that tone may be appropriate in some circumstances, it is not in keeping with the overall goal of this letter-writing

84

campaign—especially since you won't be there to clarify anything that your child misinterprets when he reads it. This letter should be about you taking responsibility for your actions and opening a dialogue, and it should be undertaken with caution, humility, and love.

In order to successfully write this letter, you need to believe that taking responsibility for your actions is the right thing to do, without any big expectation that your child will follow your lead, own his part of the conflict, or accept your apology. You need to come at this process humbly, believing that addressing this particular issue will have healing, restorative, and connecting power for your relationship with your child—*even if the change is not immediately noticed.*

The basic parts of this letter include: (1) an identified issue that will be meaningful to address, both to you and to your child, (2) an expression of how you might deal with that same situation if you had a do-over and how you think doing it differently would have impacted you both, (3) an apology for any distance your behavior might have caused, and (4) a statement of your willingness to sincerely look to the future of the relationship.

Some parents will immediately come up with one or two things that they'd like to share with their child. These moments may be ones they have regretted for years, and writing this letter will provide them the needed opportunity to begin to clear the air. However, others may look back on their relationship with their child and have difficulty coming up with anything that they'd like to set straight. If you are one of these parents, please remember this is an important letter to write—even if you do not feel that any amends need to be made. Think about what your child would like to hear as you focus some attention on a particular topic. It is possible that things that could make a big difference to your child may have seemed

> *Think about what your child would like to hear.*

very small to you at the time in comparison to things that were going on in your world. It's also possible to revisit a tough time for which you've already made amends in this letter. For example, if you have successfully recovered from a time when you and your child were at odds with each other, this letter might be a good opportunity to discuss how grateful you are that you've moved past that time and discuss where you could have done things differently from the outset.

In trying to identify a topic to write about, it might be helpful to think of two categories of actions: acts of commission and acts of omission. Acts of commission are things that you *did* that might have had (or still have) a negative impact on your relationship with your child. Some examples include:

- Discipline that was too strict, such as spankings, groundings, or restrictions of freedoms and privileges;

- Not allowing the older children (those who broke you in as a parent) to do things that the younger kids in the family are now allowed to do;

- Acknowledging the impact of your behavior (affairs, addiction, abuse, divorce) on your child;

- Emphasizing work over family time;

- Playing favorites; or

- Not believing your child when, in fact, he was telling the truth.

By contrast, acts of omission are the things that you *didn't do* that might have had or still have a negative impact on your relationship with your child. Some examples include:

- The time you felt inclined to reach out to your child but held back because you weren't sure how your gesture would be received;

- Not realizing how important a pet might have been to your child;

- Not taking that vacation you promised;

- Feeling like you should have pushed him harder in an activity, despite him saying that he wanted to quit (giving up on piano lessons or a basketball league);

- Recognizing a time when you went against your better judgment (e.g., let him only take four classes during his high school senior year); or

- Realizing that you could have done more in your marriage to avoid a painful divorce.

Once again, we can't emphasize enough the importance of this letter being very clearly written. When your child reads this letter, you won't be there to explain anything that is unclear. It might be a good idea to have a trusted person review your letter before you send it. Let this person know your objective in writing this letter is to open a dialogue with the goal of moving past an event that might be negatively impacting your relationship with your child. Listen to their feedback and make appropriate changes for clarity.

Letter Starters

- *Now that you are older, and we have moved past that time when it seemed like everything we said to each other would ignite a global conflict, I wanted to let you know that I reflect often on things I could have done differently when you were a teenager. At the time I wanted so much for us to be close, but I didn't know how to reach you.*

- *I want to share something with you that probably didn't mean that much to you at the time, but I've always considered a time in our relationship when I wish I had a "do-over." (Describe the situation and go on to talk about your experience of that time and how you'd like it to have turned out.)*

- *When I look back on those early years of me being a new father, I realize now how much I would have benefited from a "Parent's Guide to Raising Children." I placed so much emphasis on _____ that I may have missed the thing you needed from me the most.*

- *A mother's job often involves worrying about her children. I think I was really good at it. However, I never realized how much my worrying got in the way of me seeing the unique individual you are.*

- *You are probably going to think I'm blowing things out of proportion, but I feel a need to clear the air about something. I don't even know if you will remember the situation but I think about it often and regret that I didn't _____.*

Excerpts from Hindsight Is 20/20 Letters

I don't know if I ever shared with you what my life was like when you were born. The first company I worked at was big into "corporate loyalty," and the employees had to demonstrate this loyalty at every turn. It was no secret that those who sacrificed for the company were those who climbed the corporate ladder. And I climbed the ladder. I was loyal to a fault. At the time I thought that my giving to the company was really for the family, "After all," I'd tell myself, "if my job is going well then the family will have the good things in life." Well, we did have the good things. None of you kids wanted for anything. There were toys, cars, trips, and eating out, but I regret that I was at work when you took your first steps, when you said the sitter's name before you said mine, and when I missed seeing that first tooth come out. It is only now, after many years of the corporate grind that I realize that the corporation is loyal only to itself. I may have survived a downsizing here and there, but I did so at such a cost. It is hard to say what our life would be like now if I had been with a different company, and, of course, there is no guarantee that I wouldn't have still missed out on those milestones. But I wanted to let you know that time has taught me not to take for granted the opportunities I have to be with and enjoy my kids. You are one of the most important people in my life. I want you to know that my loyalty is to you and the rest of the family. I sincerely hope that you and I can start, right now, making new memories. I don't ever want to look back, in regret, on things I missed out on as you go through these next stages of your life.

* * *

This is not an easy letter for me to write because I feel I need to clear the air about something I'm not very proud of. I want to revisit something that happened in your junior year of high school. It was around the time that you were hanging out at the Jones' home a lot, and, at the time, I felt like I was losing you. In retrospect, I know that you were doing exactly what we were teaching you to do—to be independent, make decisions, and learn from the consequences—but I was just not used to you having that much freedom, and I wasn't ready for you to be on your own. Anyway, you came home later than I expected one night, and I remember going off on you. I raised my voice, threatened to ground you, took away your phone, and said things that are totally out of character for me. I was too proud to come to you the next day and ask for forgiveness for how I acted. Looking back, I am grateful that you didn't do anything hasty like run away from home (or run to the Jones' house). The weeks after were tense for both of us. We didn't speak to each other, and I know that I specifically planned on being at work later some nights so that our paths wouldn't have to cross too many times. I guess, over time we got back on track, but I missed a great deal and the chance to be an influence in your life. I regret that I was as stubborn as I was at that time, and I want to tell you that I am truly sorry for what I said and how I handled things. I am so proud of who you have become, and I look forward to seeing your life unfold. I hope that our paths can cross lots of times in the years to come. There is so much adventure ahead of you, and I'm excited to see where you take life and where life takes you. I also want you to know that I'm making a commitment to never let my pride get in the way of our relationship.

* * *

When your father and I divorced, I knew it was going to take a toll on you kids. At the time, there was no way for me to tell you all the things that were going on. Even to this day there are things about the divorce that you don't need to worry yourself about—so much of it has to be a "what's done is done" type of thing. I know that my family questioned whether I made the right choice in your father or if my youth and fantasy of what marriage should be got the best of me. I know that the divorce was certainly something I wanted. All I could see was me losing my identity in the marriage. You kids came so soon that your father and I never took the time to build our relationship, but I wouldn't change having you kids in my life for anything. Despite wanting the divorce and thinking it was the right thing to do, I wasn't prepared, and no amount of therapy could have prepared me for exactly what it was going to be like to take our family's one income and cut it in half. I cried myself to sleep on many nights second-guessing my decision and wondering just how badly it would impact you throughout your life. I don't regret my decision to divorce your father, but I think I could have handled the mechanics of it much better. You and your sister caught the brunt of my inability to keep my issues with your father to myself. I'm sure there were multiple times you got caught in the middle of our fights and disagreements. I feel horrible for that, and if there were a way to go back and change things I would—I want you to know that. The best I can do now is to make sure that I treat your father with respect and acknowledge his love for the two of you.

I'm so happy that we were both able to go to your high school graduation celebration and that it was all about you and not about either one of us or the divorce. I hope you noticed a change in how I was treating him. But even if you didn't, I need you to know that I'm so happy you are in my life. I want to commit to you that I'm doing my part to make our family a peaceful and loving group of people, even though your father and I are no longer married. You will always be special to the both of us, and I love that he loves you as much as I do. You are lucky to have two parents who love you with all their hearts. And I know that I'm lucky to have you in my life. Love you always....Mom.

This letter, if written in a thoughtful manner, can really be the source of much healing. You'll never be able to control how your child reads the letter or if your intent comes through. However, we believe that honest and sincere declarations of regret, followed by an expressed commitment to be different, are typically well received and can be powerful elements in restoring an ailing relationship or in strengthening an already healthy relationship. We encourage you to write this letter and then live up to the spirit of it. We wish you the best of luck in writing this crucial letter.

The Day You Came into My Life Letter

Kids love to hear stories about their family, and it is not only the big events they want to hear about. Of course, they want to hear stories about how Mom and Dad met, what Great-Grandpa did during the war, or what you remember about the 9/11 terrorist attacks. But merely sharing stories with facts and historical tidbits will not help your children get to know who you really are and who you are trying to become.

As children develop physically and become more mature, their capacity to understand relationships also grows, and they begin to refine their emotional intelligence (the ability to perceive, control, and evaluate emotions, or the ability to think emotionally and use emotion to connect to other human beings). They also increase their capacity to see the world more accurately, learning that adults are a mixture of virtues to be admired and flaws to be avoided. At this stage, an emotionally mature young adult begins to see parents as people who have wishes, dreams, strengths, and weaknesses, and as people who are worth getting to know better. One way to help your children know you better (and to captivate them along the way) is to let them know what was happening to you around the time they came to be in your life.

Children rarely understand the rich details about the context in which they were born.

Doing this tells them something specific and tangible about their own history, a history about which most people know very little. Sure, many people know various details about the day they were born, as related to them by their parents, but children rarely understand the rich details about the context in which they were born. Telling your children about the events surrounding their arrival in your family allows you to insert yourself into the fabric of their lives, and you become an integral part of how they think about themselves. For example, when a child knows that the story of her arrival includes details about how her birth was long-awaited and joyously anticipated, she will have a much more positive outlook toward her parents—and maybe even her purpose in life—than if the story only includes her birth weight and length.

Purpose of The Day You Came Into My Life Letter

Stories about how children come into our lives are as varied as the children themselves. Each parent has a different experience of the birth, and each child has her own unique circumstances that attended her coming into the world. This letter can be centered around the specific date she was born, the day the adoption was finalized, or even the day you decided to have a baby—the key to this letter is to make history come alive for her. Most of what you'll write to your child in this letter is information that will be largely unknown to her. While you may have already shared the time of day, the weather conditions, or the way labor went, this letter will go beyond those details to talk about you and your experience of that event. In fact, your goal is that by the time your child finishes reading this letter, she will view you as a three-dimensional person. She'll get a sense for your insecurities at the time, your love for her, and the dreams you had for your world and hers. Remember, the purpose of this letter is to open up your life to your child. Take her back in time. Let her know who you were and what it was like when you received her into your world.

Basic Elements of The Day You Came Into My Life Letter

In a broad sense, this letter is about expanding the way your child thinks about her place in the family, as well as in the world. It is also about shaping how she sees you, both for who you were and for who you've become over time. This letter can be written from a historical or metaphorical perspective—both can be equally powerful. For a historical perspective, use the details of the actual day as a framework to discuss who you were and how you felt about her. Some questions that might guide a historical approach to this letter are the following:

> *Maybe the day a child really came into your life doesn't involve a birth at all.*

- What meaning did you attach to the birth of your child?

- How did her birth change you forever?

- What were the circumstances that attended

the events of that day—was it warm or cold, rainy or snowy?

- Did the birth take place in a hospital or some other place?

- Who was present?

- Was the hospital staff supportive or difficult?

- What dramatic things happened during the procedure?

- Most importantly, what were you thinking and how were you feeling?

However, maybe the day a child *really* came into your life doesn't involve birth at all. It may have been the day you decided that being a parent was more important than having a career, or when you completed your first month of drug or alcohol treatment and made the commitment to be present in your child's life, or when the adoption was finalized. Some questions that might guide a more metaphorical approach to this letter are:

- How did you decide that your child was the most important thing in the world?

- What do you want your child to know about your love and dedication to her?

- How did family stress or relational trauma focus your attention on your role as a parent?
- What were the circumstances surrounding your decision to be an involved parent?
- What were you taught (and by whom) about being a good parent?

For this letter to have impact, it has to include details that your child may have never heard before. So, as you think about writing it, here are some topics to consider.

- Historical facts
- Personal trials and successes at the time
- Your career situation
- Your religious/spiritual views that provide meaning for her birth
- Your physical health at the time of her birth
- Your child's place in your extended family's landscape (e.g., first granddaughter)
- Significant non-family relationships
- Community influences
- Your life philosophy at the time
- Your thoughts about the role of parents

- Your personal preparation for parenthood
- Your relationship with your own parents

Letter Starters

- *It was a dark and stormy night.* (You knew we couldn't resist.)

- *I'm not sure I've ever told you about things that led up to the day you were born. While your birth itself was a routine procedure, there were other things going on for me at the time that were far from routine.*

- *The day you came into my life wasn't the day you were born. I knew you for nine months before anyone else got to see you.*

- *I think it was the Roman philosopher Cicero who said, "To remain ignorant of things that happened before you were born is to remain a child." Clearly, you are not a child anymore. It is time you knew more about the events that led to you becoming part of our family.*

- *Nine months prior to your birth, we had a blizzard that shut the town down for four days. We received 48 inches of snow in a two-day period, and the city couldn't move. The week you were born, the hospitals were so packed with "Bliz-*

zard Babies" that some women were forced to give birth in the hallways.

- *For me, there are two distinct days that you came into my life. The first is the day you were born. The second is when I completed rehab, and you were one of two people there to pick me up.*

- *I was totally unprepared to be a responsible parent when you were born.*

Excerpts from The Day You Came Into My Life Letters

I know I've already told you about the day you were born, but I recently realized that I've never really told you much about the things that were happening for me that day and around that time. It was a time when I was too young to understand what it meant to be a father. I hadn't really figured out what I was going to do with my life. I remember being outside the hospital's neonatal intensive care window looking at you—tubes and monitors all around you. It was like a scene from a movie. I kept thinking, "This is not the way it is supposed to be." I was so scared that you were going to die, and I spent hours on my knees praying to God that you'd make it past that first week. At the same time, I was secretly terrified because I believed I'd never be able to mea-

sure up to what a good father should be. I doubted that I had it in me to be capable and competent. I barely knew what I was going to do with my life, and all of a sudden I had to be a responsible adult in charge of this little life that needed so much help. You were so vulnerable. You couldn't do anything for yourself, including breathing. You needed help with everything, and I doubted my ability to be there for you.

* * *

I want you to know in no uncertain terms that your father and I worked very hard to have you in our lives. Your adoption and coming to be in our home is a story that reads like a spy novel. There were secret meetings, allegations of bribery, undisclosed conversations, greed, corruption, and deception around every corner. After three years of paperwork, assessments, interviews, and background checks, we were finally allowed to travel to Romania. At the time, the government was beginning to crack down on adoptions to the United States, and we were probably among a handful of people whose adoptions were allowed to successfully be processed that year. The path to your adoption was so difficult at times that I had to keep convincing myself that the process would be worth it in the end. The bottom line with this story, of course, is that you were wanted. We felt driven to have you in our life and knew that you would be a difference-maker in our family. Given the dramatic nature of your story, it is too hard for me not to see the hand of divine intervention in how you came to be with us.

* * *

You know how some people talk about the trauma of labor and delivery? To this day I don't know what they are referring to. People say the pain is so unbearable that it is a wonder any family has more than one child. I'm not saying that I didn't experience pain in the delivery, but I never saw it as unnatural. My body was having a normal reaction within the whole birthing process. I never wanted any drugs to take that away from me. I wanted to feel the full force of what Mother Nature intended for me to feel. From my perspective, I had had nine months to get to know you and to prepare for that day. I wasn't going to risk being drugged up and miss something spectacular. And that is just what it was—spectacular. Never before had I felt that I had a specific purpose in this world. Sure, I had done some artwork that I was proud of and that had garnered some acclaim, and I had even done some good things at work that pleased my bosses, but every accomplishment I've ever had paled in comparison to what happened that day. That day I found purpose through pain. That day you changed everything in my world.

* * *

The day you were born was also the day I was supposed to graduate from college. As you know, I took the long route toward graduation—changing my major seven times and colleges twice. I spent a lot of time being indecisive, but the day you were born there was none of that. I knew the moment I saw you that my life had changed and that I had a bigger purpose than what I wanted to be when I grow up. You changed me in an instant, and I'm a better man for it.

Beyond birth weights and weather stories are rich details of who you were as a person on the day that your child came into your life. This letter has the power to enliven the hopes and dreams your child never knew you had. She'll begin to see a new you, and she'll have questions. This letter is another invitation for your child to get to know you in all your complexity. It will open a dialogue that could change you both and refashion your relationship into one where you and your child relate to one another as adults rather than as merely parent and child.

A Picture Is Worth a Thousand Words Letter

O ne of the universals that we have discovered in our work with families is that everyone wants to know that he or she matters. People want to be noticed when they are present, and they want to be missed when absent. This is one of the reasons that teenagers work so hard to have the right clothes, hair, friends, and personality traits—so that others will notice and value them in some way. People also measure their worth based on whether or not their actions and words cause others to feel something. If they can elicit an emotion in others, then they know that they have been seen or heard. This is why we can push others to get angry or jealous, and, more importantly, this is the reason why we try to make others laugh or cry—if we can see their smile or their tears, then we know that we matter.

As this relates to your child, does he know *enough* about the times when he's made you laugh or cry? Perhaps one of these memorable moments happened on a family vacation or at a birthday party, during an award dinner, or even during an average day in the front room. No matter where it occurred, your child would love to know about it because it will remind him of how much you care. For this here we assert that a picture is worth 1,000 words—or, in other words, a good letter.

Purpose of the A Picture Is Worth a Thousand Words Letter

For this letter, we want you to find a picture that uniquely sums up a great memory you have of your child or that represents a time in your family's history, then share both the picture and your memories with your child.

For example, I (R.B.) have a picture that reminds me of a favorite memory in raising my second daughter. On the night of the movie premiere for *The Hunger Games*, I took her and three friends to a midnight IMAX showing and didn't get home until 4:00 a.m. It was a bonding experience in many ways because we had read and discussed the books, and we would both agree that the movie excursion was exhausting but totally fun.

This letter is designed to take a single moment in time and make it come alive for your child so he can remember it like it happened yesterday *and* so he can see how you remember it. It's another chance for him to get to know you. Besides, it's possible that the two of you remember different things about what was happening at the time the picture was taken. Sharing your side of the story offers him a chance to connect with you about how he remembers things, and, in the process, both of your memories become richer and more detailed.

> *Your job as a parent is to be the keeper of your child's memories.*

One of the unspoken roles of parenthood is that the parent acts as a repository of childhood memories. Many of the things kids know about themselves when they were younger are only remembered because we have told them. They don't recall their first words, the funny things they did, or the embarrassing things they said; however, once we tell them, they count those stories among their own memories. In truth, our kids are usually too busy actually living their childhood to remember many of the details. Part of your job as a parent is to be the keeper

111

of your child's memories, which makes you a very valuable commodity in the economy of the family where the currency is emotional connection. Dig through your albums, search your hard drive, and find that one picture that takes you back to all things good about your child or to the time that you both rose up and conquered something that was keeping you apart.

Basic Elements of the A Picture Is Worth a Thousand Words Letter

Begin this letter-writing project by finding a picture that you can use as your inspiration and that captures

> *Take a single moment in time and make it come alive.*

the essence of the relationship you hope to develop with your child. If you have all of your child's life already scrapbooked, then this task may take only a few minutes. If, however, you need to sort through some albums to find just the right picture, this letter may take a while. Make sure that you have plenty of time to go through your pictures. The inspirational photograph can be from a specific family outing or simply from the time period when the memorable event took place. While it is most helpful to include a photo of your favorite memory with your child, if an actual picture is unavailable, do everything you can to paint the picture in your letter so he can see what you saw through your description of that moment.

After finding your inspiration picture, prepare for writing this letter by doing the following:

- Take few minutes to sit down, away from the distractions of work, play, or media entertainment. Study the picture. Look for details that someone might not notice at first glance. The more you mention, the more your child will understand that you have devoted some time and energy to this letter. He will also realize that you have been careful in your role as a keeper of his memories.

- Use everything you can remember (and anything that others can recall) to make the picture come alive. Tell the story of what is happening in the picture so that your child can almost watch it as if it were a movie playing in his head.

- Describe what was going on the background— literally and figuratively. What else was happening in your picture? Focus on details that you can see in the picture and also present information that is only obvious to you as you think back to that time in your life. Was this a good summer when everything was going great and this moment took it to an even higher level of joy? Or was this a very difficult time in your life and this moment was a bright ray of sunshine in the middle of an emotional storm? Give him a sense of what else was happening in the world and in your family. Remember, just do the best you can—if you can't recall every detail, don't worry. Just share as much as you remember so that he knows as much as possible about himself as pictured in the photo.

- Describe any emotion that you felt as fully as you can (e.g., "I was so happy that I was smiling ear to ear"). This will help remind your child that he matters because he will be better able to imagine your emotions as he reads the letter and looks at the picture you have sent him.

Be sure to focus your letter on the most important person in the picture—your child—especially if your relationship has been strained at times. We offer this caution because, unfortunately, we have found that some parents are tempted to use this letter to present themselves as the Parent of the Year and do not give their full attention to their child. By focusing on what this picture means to you and how you believe this relates to your child, you will be less likely to write about this experience in the wrong way (e.g., rewriting the past so it favors you more, exaggerating the closeness of the parent-child bond). Finally, we recommend that you communicate this as your own personal recollection of him and/or this moment in time. This gives your child permission to remember it differently while also reminding him that you were an observer or participant in this moment as well.

Letter Starters

- *I came across this picture the other day and wanted to send it to you. You can see it was taken on our trip to Yellowstone National Park when we _____.*

- *This is one of my favorite pictures of you. I know you think it's embarrassing, but what I love about it is how totally excited you were to be _____.*

- *I've enclosed a picture I wanted you to have. I thought it was lost, but I found it when I was spring cleaning. It reminded me of how brave you were when you were in the hospital. Notice the _____.*

Seven Letters

- *If you look closely at this picture, you'll see the blur of Mom's hand in the far left corner. She was running to get out of the shot. The look on your face, beckoning to her, is priceless. What you don't know is _____.*

- *This trip to Disneyland was the one thing I wanted to make sure I was able to give you kids in your childhood years. All you cared about was the bigger-than-your-head Mickey Mouse lollipop. You hated the rides and no amount of coaxing was going to convince you to let go of that sucker.*

- *This is the only picture I have of you in your soccer uniform. I'm sending it to you, not because your one year of little league soccer was the best memory I have of you, but because it reminds me of one of the things I most admire in you.*

Excerpts from A Picture is Worth a Thousand Words Letters

This picture reminds me of one of my favorite memories—the night when we went to see the Hunger Games premiere. But it also reminds me of so many of your great characteristics. Even though you are growing up in lots of ways, this picture reminds me that you haven't lost the childlike qualities of excitement and wonder. You planned this night with your friends for weeks in terms of what you were going to wear, what you would snack on, and even what your nails would look like. You glared at the other moviegoers when you thought they weren't going to quiet down for the movie—because this was a serious moment in your young life. As the movie started, I glanced over and you somehow had a look on your face that combined complete enjoyment with a laser-like reverent focus. It made me happy to know that I had made you happy.

* * *

Son, do you remember this day? You were probably 12 or so when this picture was taken, and it was right after you swam across the lake. Before life got all complicated with serious college-level homework and adult responsibilities, this was your goal. You had tried the previous three summers, getting closer and closer each year, but I always had to pull you into the boat before you reached the other side. I knew you would be able to do it eventually, but I was still so proud when you finally did it because you didn't give up and you kept working on something that was important to you until you reached your goal. Your smile and real satisfaction shows through in the photo, even after all these years. We love you and are so proud of you today. Keep swimming and you can reach your next goal too.

Seven Letters

* * *

I love this picture and wanted to share it with you so we can remember a couple of things together. If you look close, you will notice that you and I are wearing different necklaces but everything else was matching. We were about to get family pictures taken, and I wanted us to all look good together. We fought about it for a little while but then got it worked out—you agreed to put up with the whole photo studio thing after I agreed that unicorn necklaces were stylish. One thing that I want you to remember from this is that you really are your own person and it is good to stand your ground on things that are important to you. I also want you to remember that in good relationships, people work things out by talking it out and compromising. Most importantly, I want this picture to remind you about how much I love you. We are sitting so close together in those matching outfits that it almost looks like we are wearing one big dress with two holes for our heads. Just know that I feel blessed to be your mom, and I hope that we can always be this close.

It's amazing all the meaning that can be captured in one single image. Your picture, accompanied by your words of context, will open up avenues of conversation for you and your child. Your words will change how your child views the picture and will help improve your connection—from the moment he opens your letter and every time thereafter when he sees it on his nightstand or dorm room refrigerator.

My Hopes for Your Future Letter

Being at college is like standing at a crossroads. Each path extends to an unknown future and is filled with decisions and transitions that will shape your child's life. Indeed the entire college experience is made up of transitions and changes. Almost 80% of all college students change their major at least once, and the average college student changes majors three times before graduation. Hopefully, this means that most students eventually find an academic home that leads them to a fulfilling career and that provides a good living for their future needs. However, until the time these students find that perfect fit, they may be open to suggestions and recommendations from those who are closest to them—in other words, their parents. Of course, it is important to realize that just committing to a specific major does not mean that college students have locked up the final trajectory their life will take. In fact, there is much more to having a happy and successful future than merely graduating from college, getting into a successful career, and being self-sufficient—though these things certainly help. A happy and successful future can be about so much more and you, with your considerable life experience, are in a great position to weigh in on things your child should consider.

> *The most powerful letters are letters of self-disclosure.*

If you've made it this far in this book, you know the letters you've written have had an impact on how you think about your relationship with your child and on how you see yourself as a parent. They may have also contributed to you and your student becoming closer or getting to know each other in a different way—this is certainly our hope. As we've stressed throughout the book, the most powerful letters, those that invite conversations and deepen relationships, are letters of self-disclosure, rather than lectures or nagging. This final letter can be one where you offer gentle encouragement, use your wisdom and experience to suggest things that your child should consider for her future, and tell her what your hopes are for her future.

Purpose of the My Hopes for Your Future Letter

The main purpose of this letter is, once again, to open yourself up in a way that invites connection and conversation with your child. By sharing your hopes and dreams for her future, she should feel inclined to turn to you in an attitude of thankfulness for what you've written. If she doesn't, you'll still be planting good seeds for connection in the future. Sounds pretty simple, right? It is simple, however, you will need to be careful and avoid coming across as demanding or controlling. Similarly, you don't want to put so many specific and predetermined expectations on your child that she would feel like you won't ever be pleased with her if her life turns out differently than how you've encouraged.

You also want to avoid being too specific about things that have the potential to be points of disagreement. As an example, if your college freshman is studying to be an architect, it may be a mistake for you to write that your hope for her future includes her being the best architect in the state—our architecture colleagues suggest that only half of architecture graduates actually end up as licensed architects. In fact, statements like this could have a polarizing effect between you and your child. She may begin to feel undue pressure that your happiness is somehow contingent upon her becoming an architect when she may, in fact, be considering a change of majors. So, for this letter there may be more safety in sticking with general principles and global concepts of what it means to be successful in life, as opposed to including specific details about potential career paths.

One way of avoiding traps related to specifics would be to talk about your hopes for your child's overall happiness, success, or health. It is hard to think that any child would object to your wishes for her to have a happy and healthy life. Psychologists talk about there being five dimensions of life that need to be in some sort of balance for an individual to be happy or have overall health. These dimensions are the physical, emotional, intellectual, spiritual, and social domains of life. Our lives are made up of multiple efforts and adjustments to achieve balance in these dimensions. Getting out of balance is pretty easy to do. A college student, for example, may be investing heavily in her intellectual and social dimensions, perhaps at the expense of the spiritual and physical areas. The task for her would be to appropriately allocate some time and energy to these other dimensions in order to balance out her life and give her a better chance of feeling healthy overall. Call attention how your child is doing in each of these domains. What are your hopes for her in these areas? What do you believe your child can accomplish in these domains that have eluded you in your life? What things will come easier to her than they did for you? If your letter targets any one (or all) of these dimensions and offers encouragement that she find ways to achieve balance and be happy, you'll be on the right track.

Basic Elements of the My Hopes for Your Future Letter

It is important that the overall message you give with this letter is one of positivity and hopefulness for the future. It could be very easy for your child to see this letter as one of complaint, or an essay on "How Disappointed I Am in How You've Turned Out." So, with that in mind, focus on your child's strengths and on how these attributes will contribute to her bright future. In your letter, focus on the areas where she is doing well, then transition into the areas where she seems to be struggling the most. This will help ease

> *Focus on honesty, integrity, passion, respectfulness, humility, and leadership.*

her into your letter, with your attention to her strengths buoying her up as she reads your concerns about other areas.

When thinking about your child's strengths, you might want to consider focusing on virtue-based characteristics such as honesty, integrity, passion, respectfulness, humility, and leadership. These might be characteristics you noticed early on in your child's life, or they might be qualities you've only seen hints of that you'd like to encourage with your letter. Focusing on characteristics that are unique to your child will always be well received when highlighted in a complimentary manner.

Also, even though we're suggesting this letter should avoid specific suggestions that might not be well received, we realize that you are still the parent and it is well within your role to advise and guide your child in a loving manner. So, this letter is one where you can share some of your experiences and talk about the things your experience has taught you about being happy in life. It might even be appropriate to talk about how pleased it would make you to see your child change some things about the path she is currently traveling. If you can do this in the right way, even some borderline critical or bossy recommendations may be well received. Our clinical experiences with giving people feedback on changes they should consider making in their lives suggest that if you ask for permission and shoot straight while expressing your concern, a surprising number of people will be open to the suggestions you have.

Here's an example of what we're talking about. Let's say you're not too happy with the amount of time and energy that your child has devoted to the social domain. Put more bluntly, she is spending a lot of time partying with friends at school, and you want to gently nudge her into making a change. You have already set the stage through these letters that you want to relate to her in a more adult-to-adult manner. You have praised her and remembered, with her, some incredible memories of love and connection. You have a better relationship with her than when you started this process so you can get away with saying something as bold as this:

> *"You know, one of the best things that has happened in our relationship in the last few months is that I feel like we can talk more directly, adult-to-adult. You've always been a young woman of conviction and courage, and I've seen you stand up to your peers when you thought their actions were out of line. So I'm a little worried that, right now, you've forgotten these convictions and your partying is playing a larger role in your life than*

> *it should. I think if you continue on this path it will have a negative effect on your overall happiness. Obviously, I can't make you make different decisions—you're on your own in that department. I can only tell you what it looks like from my perspective, as one who knows you well and knows what you're capable of becoming. While I'm confident you'll figure things out eventually, I do worry about how long it is taking you to do so and the many opportunities you may be missing in the meantime."*

If you have a true connection with another human being and that person believes that you ultimately have his or her best interests at heart, you'd be surprised at how bold you can be and how important your words will be to that person. We're betting that you've done the important work of connecting with your child up to this point and that a couple corrective words of wisdom in this final letter will be received with the spirit in which they were intended. If you are at all worried about whether you are writing what your child needs to hear or worried about her being able to hear you out, it might be a good idea to read this letter to her when you can gauge her ability more accurately. In this case, consider sharing this letter with her over a semester break or during a visit to campus so you can be face-to-face.

Letter Starters

- *What a great time in your life! Right now you're making decisions that will shape not only who you'll be in the future but generations to follow as well.*

- *I haven't really given any advice in these letters, but I think with this letter I want to claim a little parental privilege and make a suggestion or two about things I think you would be wise to consider. I may not know everything, but I have been around the block a time or two and hope you could benefit from my wisdom.*

- *These letters have been fun for me to write, and I hope that you've gotten a sense of who I am and that we can continue to get to know each other. I also want to let you know what my hopes are for you and your future.*

- *When I think back on the changes you've made over the past three years, and how you've been so successful in school, I get excited just thinking about the things that lie ahead of you.*

- *Despite the struggles you've been having*

in school lately, I feel confident that you'll get things figured out. You've always been resourceful in finding ways to meet your goals. Besides, school isn't the only thing there is to life. One of the things that I think makes for a happy and successful life is _____.

- *When I was younger there was no way I could have seen myself where I'm at right now. I've had several career changes and a couple different college experiences, but the things that were most important never changed—family and friends. You're fortunate to have both in abundance, and, over time, you'll come to value the role that these people can play in your life.*

Excerpts from My Hopes for Your Future Letters

This year has already been a struggle for me. I had to let my only son leave my home, and not just my home but the state as well. I can't believe how fast time has gone by and how far away you are right now. I also know that you're doing the right thing. When I look to your future, I think about the things that don't seem to change in a person. You have the same character now that you had when you were a child. You were always very tender and sweet to your younger siblings—even when they had taken something of yours without permission. I believe this trait will be something you'll call on again and again as you deal with a variety of people from all walks of life. Imagining you 20 years down the road, I see a dedicated husband, loving father, and a gentle man who is always willing to protect the innocent and less fortunate. Some young lady will be very fortunate to have you as a husband, and I think you'll be the source of inspiration to your own children and teach them many of the things you've come to learn about what makes life worth living. If there is any encouragement I could offer you, it would be to continue to be a principled person, regardless of the costs. Sometimes standing up for what is right is not always popular, but people around you will come to know what you stand for and will trust you in a variety of situations. This is what great leaders are made of, and I would not be surprised at all to see you fulfill multiple leadership roles in your life.

* * *

It's no secret that you and I have had our share of differences over the past couple of years. I appreciate how you've hung in there with me as I've begun to know you less as a child and more as an adult. It's been a hard transition for me to make, and it has caused me to think back on when I left home for college. My mom and I also struggled to see eye to eye, but we eventually got back on track, and I hope that in the coming years you and I will be able to say the same thing with our relationship. I think the thing that really helped me and my mom connect was the fact that deep down I knew that she always believed in me. When I went to college, most girls majored in home economics or education. When I told her I wanted to go into civil engineering, even though she was freaking out on the inside, she looked me in the eye and told me that she knew I'd do great at it. On more than one occasion, when things were tough and the chauvinists in my class—including the professors—were looking down their noses at me and telling me to drop out, I would remember that vote of confidence that your grandmother gave me. It kept me going.

I hope that in some small way I, too, can be an influence in your life and let you know that you can accomplish great things. I have every confidence that you'll push limits and challenge the system at your school. I know you're going to make me proud. The other day I saw someone wearing a t-shirt that read, "Well-behaved Women Seldom Make History" and I thought of you. When I look at your future, I think you have the potential to make history, and if not history, at least a significant impact on the lives of those you touch. I'm so happy that you got to be in my home and that I get to be your mom for years to come.

* * *

When I began writing these letters I wasn't really sure what effect they would have on our relationship, but my hope was that it would help bring us closer together. Through the letters, I'm realizing that I've waited much too long to say some of the things to you that I've now said in the past couple of months. I was never one to do too much self-talk, but when I hold back parts of me, I now understand that it makes it harder for you to get to know me and allow me to have some space in your life. In that way, I see a lot of similarities between you and me. You were never really one to give me any details about what was going on in your life. If there is one thing I would wish for your future it is that you would learn earlier than me how important it is to share yourself with the people that are close to you. I know it will be a challenge because it'll be like using muscle groups that have been inactive for so long.

I'm not sure that relationships just flow for you and I the way they do for your sister or your mom. We just seem to be cut from different cloth than them. When I look back on the divorce from your mother, I now realize (with the help of a little therapy and life experience) that it might have been a different ending if I had learned how to let you guys into my life more than I was capable of doing back then. I worry a bit that this might be a lesson that you, too, will learn only after much pain and heartache. Obviously things have worked out in the long run. Your mom and I treat each other civilly, we're both in healthy relationships, and we both love you kids. However, I just wish someone had told me a bit more about how to open up and let people into my life. I was always so worried that if I let people in, they'd turn around and hurt me. I now realize that letting people in does expose me to that risk, but it also allows me the opportunity to really be connected to other human beings, which is something that is so valuable to me.

We have confidence that your words of gentle encouragement or even those of admonishment will help your child see you in a new light. By using your wisdom and experience in telling her your hopes for her future, you open yourself up and invite connection and conversation. This will also be a letter that your child will read and re-read, it may be the type of letter that helps them see one path more clearly than others. This letter, and all that you hope for your child's future, represent the epitome of being an involved and caring parent.

This is the final letter that we're offering you guidance with. From here on out, you'll make the decisions about any future letters that you want to write and send. It is our sincere hope that you will find yourself in a better position to connect with your child in an adult-to-adult manner after completing this letter-writing campaign and that these seven letters have truly brought you closer to your college-student.

A Final Word

A re you more likely to turn to the back of a magazine and read it from there? Maybe you like to know what will happen to the hero and villain before you get introduced to them at the beginning of a book. Regardless, this final chapter is dedicated to all the "from the back first" readers out there, those who need some idea of the outcome before deciding to invest in this process. Not a bad idea in this case, because, after all, we're asking you to invest in a letter-writing campaign that is designed to bring you closer to your child.

To sum up, we have designed the exercises in this book to coach a parent through an intentional process of self-disclosure. We continue to believe that as you push yourself to be more open and honest, your child will come to respect your efforts and recognize how much you care. We have encouraged you to consider the possibility that strengthening your relationship with your child can be as simple as writing seven heartfelt letters. Each of these seven letters has a specific theme that works toward the same purpose: to invite further conversation, enhance a mutual understanding, and foster a deeper emotional connection between parents and their college-age children. The themes of each of the letters are as follows:

- **The Suitcase Letter:** Slipped into your student's bag before you say goodbye, the Suitcase Letter helps set the tone for your student's first weeks at school and addresses the excitement of beginning college, the characteristics that will help her in school, and your confidence that she will succeed. It also sets the stage for the remaining letters and begins to redefine how the two of you relate.

- **Letter of Praise:** A thoughtful Letter of Praise highlights your child's admirable internal qualities and past successes. It can help him see his strengths and his accomplishments as both real and valuable and can serve as a buffer against the difficulties he will face in college.

- *Family Legacy Letter:* Drawing on your heritage and family history—the good and the bad—the Family Legacy Letter sends a strong message of encouragement, teaches character lessons, and reinforces your faith in your child's potential. Properly written, your legacy can inspire and direct a young adult struggling to figure out her place in the world.

- *Hindsight is 20/20 Letter:* The Hindsight Is 20/20 Letter provides an opportunity for you to take responsibility for a past action that may have harmed your relationship with your child. The goal of this letter is simply to open a dialogue. If written in a thoughtful manner, this letter can provide powerful healing to an ailing relationship and be a great source of strength for a healthy one.

- *The Day You Came Into My Life Letter:* An invitation for your child to get to know you in all your complexity, the Day You Came Into My Life Letter shares rich details of who you were and introduces your child to you as a three-dimensional person with hopes, dreams, insecurities, and weaknesses. This new perspective can help your child relate to you on more of an adult-to-adult level.

- *A Picture is Worth a Thousand Words Letter:* Relying on the adage that "a picture is worth 1,000 words," this letter gives context to a single moment in time, using a picture to discuss your memories and to send a positive message to your child. It opens up new avenues of conversation and provides another chance for him to get to know you.

- *My Hopes for Your Future Letter:* Focusing on your child's strengths and offering gentle encouragement, this final letter builds on the good will the previous letters will have generated between you and your child. It offers you the opportunity to gently express your hopes for your child's future and offer advice to help her find happiness in life.

We started this book with the simple belief that, regardless of geographic distance or how old the child may be, a parent can always be a significant source of affirmation and guidance to their child. We believe that writing these specific letters and communicating with your child like you've never done before will have a dramatic impact on your relationship. Hopefully, your child will come to know you in a different way, seeing a depth and humanity in you that he's never seen before. Hopefully, your child has begun to see that you're much more than the person he had believed you to be.

Having successfully written the letters is a testimony of your dedication to and investment in your child and reflects your interest in developing a more meaningful connection with your child. You are to be congratulated for even thinking about taking on a task like this, let alone completing it. With this experience under your belt, you may decide that your relationship with your other children—or even your spouse or members of your extended family—could benefit from your writing a specific letter. Perhaps one of your adult siblings needs an opportunity to reconnect through a similar letter writing exercise, or you might decide that a church or community leader whose support has meant a lot to you would appreciate a handwritten letter much more than an email. You can do so now, knowing that the letter-writing process you've undertaken is based on principles that help to develop and strengthen emotional bonds with other human beings. We have learned these principles in over 40 years of combined experience helping family members connect with one another. We believe that engaging in a process of open and honest self-disclosure with people we love is a cornerstone for developing and strengthening human relationships. Doing so through handwritten letters provides a novel, nostalgic and lasting way to extend this invitation to those we love. We've seen it work before as we've counseled parents and college students in university orientation meetings and family therapy sessions; we believe it will work for you.

We wish you the best of luck and would love to hear your success stories.

Warmest Regards,
Steve Harris & Roy Bean